THE
FORTHBRINGER
OF GOD

St Bonaventure on the Virgin Mary

By
George H. Tavard

FRANCISCAN HERALD PRESS
1434 West 51st Street • Chicago, Illinois 60609

THE FORTHBRINGER OF GOD: St Bonaventure on the Virgin Mary by George H. Tavard. Copyright © 1989 by Franciscan Herald Press, 1434 West 51st Street, Chicago, Illinois 60609. All rights reserved.

Library of Congress Cataloging-in-Publication Data

Tavard, George H. (George Henry), 1922-
    The forthbringer of God : St Bonaventure on the Virgin Mary / by George H. Tavard.
        p. cm.
    ISBN 0-8199-0924-6
    1. Mary, Blessed Virgin, Saint—History of doctrines—Middle Ages, 600-1500.   2. Bonaventure, Saint, Cardinal, ca. 1217-1274—Contributions in Mariology.   I. Title.
BT610.T33 1988
232.91'092'4—dc19   88-23350
                                                                CIP

Cover design by William Dichtl & Blane O'Neill, O.F.M.

MADE IN THE UNITED STATES OF AMERICA

CONTENTS

FOREWORD

The present volume grew out of the Dialogue between Lutherans and Roman Catholics in the USA, though I am solely responsible for its contents. Since February 1984, this dialogue has been studying, as thoroughly as possible, the pending problems between the Lutheran and the Roman Catholic traditions on the subject of the Virgin Mary, her relationship to Christ, her position in God's plan of salvation, her place in Christian dogma and piety. Having agreed to prepare, for the meeting of February 1986, a paper on the theology of St Bonaventure (1221-1274) on the Virgin Mary, as compared with that of the other great Franciscan doctor, John Duns Scotus (1266-1308), I was constrained by the abundance of material to restrict my study of Bonaventure to his main scholastic work, the *Commentary on the Sentences,* and my investigation of Duns Scotus to his position on the Immaculate Conception. For my own enlightenment, however, I also read Bonaventure's other works, with which I have been familiar for a long time, in their relevant Marian passages. While looking at secondary literature, I was puzzled that Bonaventure had clearly been eclipsed by Duns Scotus in that historical and theological scholarship, even among Franciscan authors, has paid much more attention to the Subtle Doctor than to the Seraphic Doctor. The reason for this is, presumably, that Bonaventure denied the Immaculate Conception of Mary, whereas Duns Scotus was the one whose argument in favor of the doctrine eventually obtained the consensus of Roman Catholic theologians. As a result of this, and no doubt also under the influence of a developing popular devotion to Mary, the doctrine of the Immaculate Conception was dogmatically defined, a first time at the thirty-sixth session of the Council of Basle, September 17, 1438, a second time—the Council of Basle not having been received as ecumenical—by Pope Pius IX on December 8, 1854.

The assumption that Bonaventure is not worth studying because he did not share the later position of John Duns Scotus would seem to be hasty. After all, Bonaventure shared his opinion with St Bernard and St Thomas Aquinas! Be that as it may, it should be worthwhile to understand a perspective on the Virgin Mary which antedates the formulation of the later Marian dogmas. The ecumenical question, prominent today, urges all Christian believers to review the points where Catholics and Protestants have differed with both eagerness and sincerity. The place of the Virgin Mary in doctrine and piety is one of these points of divergence. Is it not possible that a better knowledge of the older Marian tradition of the Catholic Church may suggest insights on how the contemporary hurdles may be by-passed? This at least has been the hope in which I have composed the present work.

The four parts of this book follow the pattern of Bonaventure's theological writings. When he was a student and a professor at the university of Paris, he began, as was usual at the time, with theological investigations relating to Peter Lombard's *Sentences*: hence part one, *Theology*. He also, in a parallel way, worked at several biblical commentaries, in which he spent considerable time on St Luke's account of the Annunciation: this is my part two, *Scriptural Meditation*. Besides studying theology and Scripture, Bonaventure preached abundantly, and many of his sermons have been preserved. A number of these were pronounced on the feasts of the Virgin Mary: whence part three, *Liturgical Piety*. Having been forced, once elected to head the Order of St Francis, to relinquish scholastic teaching, Bonaventure composed a number of short works on the spiritual life and, in the last years of his life, three series of special theological lectures in a non-scholastic mode: these are covered in my fourth part, *Mystical Insight*.

There may be several ways to read this book. Readers who would use it for edification will lose little by starting with chapter 3. As they deal with scholastic questions, some of which are no longer prominent in modern theology, the first two chapters will be considered superfluous or arduous by many, though they will be essential to those who are interested in the historical development of Catholic Mariology. Students who would read this book for a course in Christology or Mariology may wish to start with part two, since contemporary seminary courses often begin with a biblical enquiry of their topic. Preachers or liturgists may find it useful to start with part three. Finally, a word on the title is in order. The expression, "Forthbringer of God," is not common in Catholic piety. But it corresponds more strictly than the familiar "Mother of God" to the Greek term, *Theotocos,* and to the Latin expressions which translate it, *Dei Genitrix* and *Deipara.* It evokes exactly the aspect of the divine motherhood which is the most emphasized by Bonaventure: in her task as channel of the Incarnation, Mary brought forth to us the Word of God incarnate. As this already suggests, the heart of Bonaventurian Mariology is to be found in his recurrent reflections on the Annunciation.

I dedicate this work generally, in an ecumenical spirit, to all the Christian believers who feel respect and veneration for the Virgin Mary, Mother of Christ, Forthbringer of God, and who share with St Bonaventure and the older theologians their disagreement with the modern Catholic doctrine of the Immaculate Conception.

Part One

Theology

CHAPTER I

INTIMATIONS

Bonaventure embarked on his theological career around the year 1245, writing down notes that could eventually serve for a full-size commentary on the Sentences of Peter Lombard, a task that was required of all professors of theology in the thirteenth century. What has been preserved of these notes has received the unfortunate title, *dubia circa litteram*, that is, "doubts, or questions, concerning the letter" of Peter Lombard's Sentences. It has been dispersed, in the standard edition, throughout the Commentary which he composed a few years later.[1] These notes are occasional, not systematic; exploratory, not definitive. They are not entirely original, since they closely reflect the teaching of Bonaventure's masters. They especially underline his indebtedness to Alexander of Hales (d. 1245), who had been the first Franciscan to teach at the University of Paris. (He was in fact already a recognized authority at the university when he joined the Order of St Francis).

Such as they are, however, these notes remain precious. For they give us the first version of their author's thinking on many points of theology. Only a few relate to the Virgin Mary; but they sufficiently point out the direction which the doctrine of Bonaventure of Bagnoregio was taking in his apprenticeship of a professorial career. They will provide us with material for a preliminary enquiry into his views on the holy Virgin.

* * * * *

There are two aspects to the image of Mary in Christian thought and piety. On the one hand, as a daughter of the Jewish people and as the inhabitant of an obscure village of Galilee, she is one of us, an unpretentious member of the human race. We can empathize with her in the hardships or simply in the normal events of her life as a young girl, a fiancée, a mother. On the other hand, she was raised above all of us and even above the angels by the very dignity of her Son, Jesus of Nazareth, whom faith knows as the Son of God, the divine Word who became flesh in her for the salvation of humankind.

As one of us, Mary is indeed our neighbor. "By the word, neighbor, one understands every human person of either sex, of whatever dignity, of whatever virtue. Whence love for the glorious Virgin is included under love for the neighbor."[2] Mary is "next to us in conformity of nature"; and love—"dilection"—is always related to similarity. Our love therefore goes to the Virgin, not because she is to be venerated or for the graces she received from God, but simply because she is one of us. This of course does not rule out the veneration to which her mission entitles her. She is indeed "above us," due to "the dignity of grace and of the most noble conception" of her Son. Veneration of her ranks higher than that of any other saint. Yet neither love nor veneration for her threatens the proper order of charity: "However much a creature is to be loved with great affection, the order of charity requires the soul to love its own salvation first."

It was as one of us that Mary, reacting as a woman does to her dear ones' pains, was saddened and afflicted by the Passion of her Son. But, as Bonaventure points out, such affliction can be channelled in two ways. First, one can wish for the opposite of the divine will. This way was followed by Peter when, in Matthew, 16:23, he was confronted with the prophecy of the Passion of Jesus. Peter was duly reproved for his attitude. Second, another way is open when

> sadness for another person carries us, by the will of piety, to the contrary [of what we would like], yet nonetheless this contrary is willed positively. It is good to suffer thus with Christ and to feel piously affected on his behalf; thus have the saints been affected when they gave thanks to God for the passion of Christ; yet they are piously moved by the consideration of his sufferings.[3]

This was the Virgin's way at the cross: "The pious soul of the blessed Virgin suffered with her most beloved and suffering Son, as much as she could bear." In this "the Mother was entirely in conformity with the Father," willing to "exchange the Only-Son for the salvation of humankind."

On account of her acceptance of God's will,

> she should be admirably praised and loved, for it
> pleased her that her Only-Son be offered for the
> salvation of the human race. She felt so much com-
> passion that, had it been possible, she would willingly
> have taken on herself all the torments born by her
> Son. She was strong and pious, gentle and steadfast,
> strict with herself and most generous with us. She
> is therefore to be principally loved and venerated
> after the supreme Trinity and her most blessed
> offspring, Jesus Christ our Lord.

* * * * *

The Virgin Mary was married. But what sort of marriage
was it? Since marriage is made, first of all, by the two
partners' mutual consent, one may properly ask, in view
of the Christian assertion of her virginity, to what she
consented when she agreed to marry Joseph of Nazareth.
Did she consent to sexual union?

Behind this question, as it is formulated in IV, d. 30,
dub. 5, there is a reference to a passage from St Augustine,
in which an objector finds Mary's marriage inconsistent,
on the ground that consent to marriage naturally implies
consent to sexual union. Bonaventure's answer is simply
that Mary did not consent to be sexually known, "since
I do not believe that she wanted it or that God inspired
it to her."[4] Rather, she consented "to conjugal society or
to the mutual property of their bodies, which is ordered
to sexual union, but not with necessary order." In other
words, there is no contradiction in assenting to a non-

consumable marriage if the partners are in agreement.

Other problems are raised by some passages in the Gospels. Two texts are examined briefly. Does Matthew, 1: 24 imply that "after" (*donec*) the birth of her "firstborn," Mary had other children? Bonaventure identifies this interpretation of Scripture as "the heresy of the Claudians,"[5] and he is not soft with what he perceives as a heresy. It is, as he says, "totally irrational that the most blessed Mother of God, after being the temple of God and of the Holy Spirit, would have performed the work of the flesh. To believe such an indignity of the Mother of God can only enter a soul that is impious and stupid; therefore it is erroneous and pernicious." Further, the words of Jesus to the beloved disciple and to Mary ("This is your mother . . . This is your son") in John 19: 26-27, imply that Mary had no son of her own left to comfort her. Then, "firstborn" simply denotes the time when the event in question took place; it refers to the past (no one came before), leaving the future outside the perspective. Moreover, the term "brothers" in the Gospels can designate "cousins in the second or third degree." One may remark that this is in fact the common practice in societies centered on the extended family. Only in the modern world of the twentieth century is the nuclear family the rule.

The Annunciation is of course the fundamental episode in the New Testament account of the Mother of the Lord. Even in the sketchy Marian perspective of these first notes of theology, Bonaventure already speaks of it. The question which is asked may not strike us today as of major import, yet it retained his attention: Why was the Incarnation announced by an angel?

At the most interesting point of his answer, Bonaventure argues, without using the term, from a notion which derives from the *Epistle to the Ephesians*, 1:10, as interpreted theologically by St. Irenaeus before the end of the second century, namely, recapitulation. To recapitulate something is to restore it and put it in a new key by giving a new orientation or meaning to past events that are now relived in a fresh way. For Irenaeus, this new way reverses the old, thus changing the course of history. The events in question are those of the temptation of Eve by the evil angel in the garden of Eden, contrasted with the good angel's message to Mary. In the light of the Annunciation, one may say that

> the order of reparation would correspond to the order of prevarication. Hence, as the devil tempted a woman to bring her into doubt, and through doubt to consent, and through consent to the fall; so the angel announced to the Virgin, that by this Annunciation she would be brought to faith, and by faith to consent, and by consent to the conception of the Son of God through the Holy Spirit.[6]

An additional idea is that the Virgin, being still on the pilgrim way of this life while the angel is already in eternal blessedness, the angel knew God's will better than she did. Again: the angel at the Annunciation acted as a servant to his lady, for he was "God's servant and minister," sent to her who was "elected and preelected to be the Mother of God." Furthermore, redemption, as Bonaventure understands it, was to be done through a man, Jesus. But it would also include angels as well as women and men. It was therefore proper that angels, like women, be not excluded from knowing "the mystery of the Incarnation and even of the Resurrection. Moreover, God announces both, through an angel, to a woman, the Incarnation to the blessed Virgin, and the Resurrection to Magdalen." Bonaventure also specifies that at the moment of the Annunciation "the Virgin Mary was nearer to God than the angel . . . as to the grace of election, but not as to the grace of comprehension." That is, although preelected to be the Mother of God, she still walked by faith only.

* * * * *

This opens a perspective on Mary's superiority. While she is indeed one of us, she is also above us. The principle of this superiority can be seen from three angles, relating to the "grace of conception," the "grace of justification," that of any other woman, since no higher conception can be imagined. "If all creatures, whatever their degree of imagined. "If all creatures, whatever their degree of nobility, were present, they all would owe reverence to the Mother of God."[7] The second grace was the highest that could be received by a mere creature. As to Mary's natural endowments, she had all that was needed for her purpose and mission. A scale of grace results from this. Christ stands at the top, with his human nature's capacity for divine grace completely filled. His Mother follows, her grace being as much as "a mere rational creature of the feminine sex can have of what pertains to her body, and in her human soul of what pertains to grace." Finally, there are other men and women, whose "capacity for grace

God filled," but with lesser capacities.

Mary's superiority over the usual human condition, which she nevertheless shares in everything else, includes the fact that, by grace, she was preventively freed from sin. Unlike other humans, therefore, the Virgin had no need for the stimulus of concupiscence or disorderly desire. This is useful to our "fallen and sick nature," which it introduces to the humility of human self-knowledge before God. But to her this would have been superfluous, since she was "filled with charity and humility, and confirmed in both."[8] It is for this reason that, at the Annunciation, the presence of the Most High is called an overshadowing rather than an illumination: "Overshadowing cools the heat, and in the coming of the Son of God the Virgin was cooled by the extinction of concupiscence in her."[9] Further, she was "assisted toward the contemplation of God by the union of her flesh with the Word, so that, being unable to feel God in herself because of the immensity of his light, she could feel and know him in herself through the assumed humility of his flesh." What Bonaventure is suggesting here is simply that the Annunciation, and the ensuing state of the Virgin as she bore the Son of God, were of the rank and quality of the highest mystical states. She was, then, as profoundly united to God as is possible to anyone in this life. But this union did not yet take place in the light of the eternal vision of God. Mary was in the darkness of faith, in "the humility of her flesh." Only by a special gift from divine grace, not by her own deeds and merits could the Virgin say that she had no sin. In her alone of all humankind the concupiscence that derives from original sin was extinguished. "For the entire time of her life she committed no actual sin, which can truly be said of no other saint, whatever the length of his life."[10]

Mary also, though "merely a creature, has been raised above the angels."[11] This notion may be disconcerting to the modern mind, for which belief in angels has the colors of an oddity. Yet Bonaventure insists on it, partly because of the important place of angels in his overall vision of the created universe, partly because of his conviction that Christ is the Savior of the good angels as much as he is the Redeemer of humanity. Precisely, it was also as Son of God that Christ came to the angels. Since he is therefore honored by them as the Son of Mary, it is normal that his Mother should also receive veneration and respect from the angels. Gabriel was her servant at the Annunciation. If one conceives of heaven as having higher and lower levels, or—in keeping with the cosmography of the ancients—as made of several successive heavens (nine, in Bonaventure's reckoning), then the highest is the "heaven of the Trinity,"[12] which is also that of the human nature of Christ, sitting at the right hand of the Father. "After him we believe the blessed Virgin to be above the others," whether angels or humans. "Afterwards the others rank according to their merits." Since, however, one can hardly imagine heaven and its hierarchy, "it is more to be desired than to be described with an image."

* * * * *

These scattered notes do not of course add up to a full treatment of the place of Mary in the Christian faith. Bonaventure is only beginning, with the help of the great masters who were the first Franciscan teachers in Paris, his theological reflection. Mary will have her place in this, in keeping with the scholastic method of reflection on the work of Peter Lombard.

Notes

1. The standard edition of his works is, *Opera Omnia . . .* , 10 vol., (Quaracchi, Italy: Collegio S. Bonaventurae, 1882-1902). The commentary occupies vol. 1-4. I have generally used the desk edition, *Opera Theologica Selecta*, 4 vol., (Quaracchi, 1934-1949). On Bonaventure's life and works, see Guy Bougerol, *Introduction to the Works of Bonaventure*, (Chicago, IL: Franciscan Herald Press, 1964); on his philosophical background: John F. Quinn, *The Historical Constitution of St Bonaventure's Philosophy*, (Toronto: Institute of Medieval Studies, 1973); on his Christology: Zachary Hayes, *The Hidden Center, Spirituality and Speculative Christology in St Bonaventure*, (New York: Paulist, 1981).

2. II, d. 28, dub. II.

3. I, d. 48, dub. IV.

4. IV, d. 30, dub. V.

5. IV, d. 30, dub. IV. The "Claudians" were followers of the opinions of Claudius of Turin (d. 829), a bishop who condemned the use of holy pictures and the veneration of saints, in a book, *De Imaginibus Sanctorum*.

6. III, d. 2, dub. IV.

7. I, d. 44, dub. IV.

8. III, d. 3, p. 1, dub. I.

9. l. c., dub. II.

10. l. c., dub. IV.

11. I, d. 16, dub. III.

12. II, d. 2, p. 2, dub. II.

CHAPTER 2

THEOLOGICAL INVESTIGATIONS

Nowhere in Bonaventure's Commentary on the Sentences is there a systematic tractate on the Virgin. The main discussion of Marian questions occurs in book III, in relation to the Incarnation. The order of the material is determined by Bonaventure's perception of how Peter Lombard presented the traditional doctrine concerning Christ. The logic is therefore Christological. The questions are indeed quite specific; and the answers may go into more details than contemporary authors would deem necessary. This very specificity may be misleading, in that it does not stress the methodological context in which such questions are asked. Bonaventure defines his theological method as being both theocentric and Christocentric.[1] It is "radically" theocentric: "God himself" is the principle of all that theology deals with. It is also "integrally" Christocentric: the subject matter of theology is "integrally" in Christ, even though, "universally," it comes to us in the sacramental or quasi-sacramental form of the articles of faith. The point, for our investigation, is that Bonaventure's specific questions about Mary, even when they are not referred directly to Christ and the Incarnation, do pertain, in Bonaventure's perspective, to Christ as the "integral" subject matter of theological reflection. Thus the logic and the context of Bonaventure's considerations on Mary are Christological.

To order the questions according to a Mariological logic, one may say that Bonaventure speaks successively of Mary's sanctification and holiness (d. 3), of her "merit" and "cooperation" with God in the conception of Christ (d. 4), of the title *Dei Genitrix* or (in Greek) *Theotokos* (d. 4, a. 3, q. 3; d. 8), of the cult of Mary (d. 8), of Mary's virginity (d. 12) and, again, of her holiness (d. 15).[2] For simplicity's sake, I will group the topics of the present chapter under three headings: 1° Holiness, including the question of Mary's merit; 2° the title, *Theotocos*, including —for reasons that will emerge—the question of Mary's cooperation with God in the Incarnation; 3° virginity. I will borrow the general framework of this chapter from book III, adding elements from the other books of the Commentary as will be appropriate. Consideration of the cult of Mary will be left for a later chapter.

Holiness

This receives by far the most attention and the longest treatment. D. 3 is structured as follows:

d. 3, p. 1: "The blessed Virgin's sanctification."

a. 1: "The Virgin's sanctification as to its congruous moment (*quoad congruentiam temporis*)."

q. 1: "Whether the Virgin's flesh was sanctified

before being animated."

q. 2: "Whether the blessed Virgin's soul was sanctified before contracting original sin."

q. 3: "Whether the blessed Virgin was sanctified before her birth."

a. 2 "The effectiveness of this sanctification."

q. 1: "Whether the blessed Virgin by the grace of sanctification was immune to all actual sin."

q. 2: "Whether in her first sanctification concupiscence was extinguished in the Virgin."

q. 3: "Whether in her second sanctification the power to sin was removed from the blessed Virgin."

Q. 1 examines two main points. The wisdom of celebrating Mary's conception (not "immaculate," but plain ordinary conception) is examined in relation to some unnamed persons' view that Mary was sanctified in her flesh before receiving a soul.[3] As Bonaventure shows, this opinion implies a contradiction, since the grace of sanctification presupposes a soul as the medium through which it is given. Such a mediating soul could not be her parents', for three reasons. Firstly, an offspring "is not in the parents as to its soul"; secondly, sanctification, like original justice in Adam, could not be channelled by a "libidinous coitus, because two contraries would then be together and at the same time in one thing"; thirdly, her parents could not share "a prerogative that belongs only to the holy Virgin: she alone, as the saints say, conceived without sin and gave birth without pain" (c.).

A most interesting discussion is found in a liturgical excursus, in *ad* 4. The Holy Spirit, Bonaventure specifies, acts sometimes as Spirit, sometimes as Holy. As Spirit he performs miracles, and he could have made sure that, Mary's parents being old and her mother sterile, her conception took place without *libido*, though this would not have impeded the transmission of original sin. As Holy, the Spirit sanctifies. In John the Baptist's conception, he acted only as Spirit; in Mary's, he acted also as Holy. But is this a sufficient reason to celebrate Mary's conception liturgically?

Some people do so "out of special devotion, whom I dare neither praise entirely nor simply reprove." It cannot be approved entirely since great devotees of the Virgin, like St Bernard, condemned it: the "statutes of the universal Church for the feasts of saints are all founded on sanctification, so that it [the Church] solemnizes no day in honor of any saint, in which or for which the person to whom this honor is offered was not holy. If therefore holiness was not in the Virgin before her soul's infusion, it does not seem completely safe to celebrate the solemnity of her conception."

Yet Bonaventure dared not condemn such a celebration. He is impressed by the claim that the feast was started "not by human invention, but by divine revelation."[4] He also suspects that the point of the feast may well be Mary's future sanctification rather than her actual conception. Hence his hesitant conclusion:

> I believe, however, and I trust, concerning the glorious Virgin, that if someone celebrates this feast, not for novelty's sake, but out of devotion to the Virgin, without believing anything contrary to what can be elicited from Holy Scripture, the blessed Virgin accepts this devotion; and if there is something

reprehensible, I hope that it will be excused by the just Judge.

Besides, Bernard's main concern was not to curb devotion, but to make sure that "no one believes that the Virgin was sanctified in her conception." In any case the other saints will not be envious of the Virgin if "the power and the speed of her sanctification surpass the others." Bonaventure finally appeals to experience:

It is not surprising that the Holy Spirit, dwelling in the hearts of the faithful, should inflame their devotion to the Virgin more than to other saints. . . . Therefore, at whatever time, on whatever day, some of the faithful honor the Virgin with all their heart and soul, they should not be harshly reproved, lest one incur the displeasure of the Virgin, who helps and loves all the faithful who praise her, as these have known it in a multitude of ways.

* * * * *

Q. 2, a thorough discussion of the problem of the Immaculate Conception, should be analyzed in some detail, owing to its importance. The opinions pro and con which precede the center of Bonaventure's answer begin with the description of six approaches that have been used to promote the doctrine of Mary's Immaculate Conception:
1° Anselm (*De conceptu virginis*, 18) taught that Mary enjoyed a purity "than which no greater under God can be conceived." This can only be a sanctification before

inheriting original guilt.

2° Augustine (*De natura et gratia*, 36) excepted Mary from the consideration of sins.

3° John of Damascus (*De fide orthodoxa*, IV, 16) wrote that "the Mother's honor is referred to the Son." As the Son deserves the greatest honor in regard to freedom from sin, so the Mother must have been "immune to all guilt, original as well as actual."

4° A reason from philosophy or esthetics suggests that there ought to be a mean where there are two extremes. The extremes being, on the one side, "the sons of Adam," with original sin in both their soul and their flesh, and, on the other, Christ, who has no sin at all, a third party ought to have original sin "in the flesh but not in the soul": this is the Virgin Mary. (A fourth position—in the soul but not in the flesh—would be self-contradictory, therefore impossible).

5° A theological principle holds that "the Virgin's sanctification exceeds that of the other saints." As the greatest of these, John, was sanctified "in his birth from the womb," the Virgin must have been sanctified both "from and in the womb." But "the birth in the womb is the soul's infusion; therefore at the first moment of her soul's infusion, the Virgin had the holiness of divine grace; therefore she never had the infection of original guilt."

6° It is proper (*congruum*) to posit that God gave the Virgin what it was proper (*congruebat*) for her to receive." Since it was proper for her to be given "original grace at the first moment," one should hold that she was exempt from original sin.

Six arguments are then listed against the Immaculate Conception. Bonaventure does not necessarily approve them all; they serve chiefly to highlight the liveliness of the debate in the mid-thirteenth century:

a° Paul in Rom 5:12, asserts: "All in Adam sinned . . ."

b° Augustine (*De correptione et gratia*, 7, 11) wrote: "No one is freed from the mass of damnation except in the Redeemer's faith."

c° Reason indicates that if the Virgin had no original sin she did not deserve to die. In this case, either her death was unjust or it contributed to salvation. But both are impossible, for then either God would be unjust or Christ would not be "a sufficient Redeemer." One may remark here that this touches on the doctrine of the Assumption, as it assumes that Mary died;[5] and it also denies all co-redemption.

d° Had Mary never had original sin, she should not have died; or if she died, her death should have served the salvation of humankind. But the first case would be injurious to God (who then would have been unjust in letting her die); and the second would be injurious to Christ (who then would not be the only redeemer).

e° No one who is without sin belongs to Christ's redemption. And, as his glory is to redeem the saints, Christ would be deprived of glory if he had not redeemed Mary.

f° Had Mary no original sin, she would have reached heaven before Christ if she died first; but this would imply that "the gate of heaven was not opened by Christ for all," in contradiction to *Colossians 1:19*.

In the corpus of the question, Bonaventure explains at length and with sympathy the position of those who attribute to the Virgin some sort of immaculate conception. Yet he also accumulates arguments that invalidate such a doctrine.

"Some have wished to say that in the soul of the glorious Virgin the grace of sanctification preceded the stain of original sin." This, as Bonaventure understands it, is supported by a central reason and also by "multiple congruency."

The central reason has to do with the Virgin's superiority to the other saints in regard to the effectiveness of grace in her. She must be above the saints not only in "abundance of holiness" but also in "acceleration of time." In her case, the Holy Spirit, working above what nature does, shortened the normal course of time. "Therefore at the instant of her creation, grace was infused in her; and at the same instant her soul was infused in the flesh." Because "wisdom is faster than all that is fast" (Wis 7:24), and "grace is much more powerful than nature," the effect of grace was "faster in her flesh than the effect of evil in her soul." I take this evil to be original sin as communicated by her parents in the normal way of conception. The situation would be that original sin was in fact communicated to her but was never received by her because grace acted faster than nature.

The multiple congruence on the side of such a doctrine relates to "the honor of Christ," to the prerogative by which the Virgin "must come before other male and female saints by the dignity of her sanctification," and to "the beauty of order," that is, the esthetic point of view which looks for a mean between extremes. Between a person (Christ) who is free from original sin in both flesh and soul, "that is, in the cause and the effect," and one (Adam) who is subject to it both in flesh and in soul, there ought to be "a median person, who somehow would have it and somehow would not have it; and this is the blessed

Virgin who is Mediatrix between us and Christ as Christ is between us and God." It is clear that, at this point, the word *Mediatrix* does not denote intercession or mediation of grace; it simply describes the median position of one who stands in the middle between two others. Further congruence is found in Anselm's quotation from arg. 1.

Those who favor this opinion maintain that it respects "the truth of sacred Scripture and of the Christian faith." The biblical argument is typological: the Virgin's soul is signified by the urn in which manna (grace) was deposited in the ark (flesh): the urn did receive manna before being placed in the ark; likewise the soul of Mary before being placed in her body. . . . Moreover the Christian faith is respected, since "the Virgin was freed from original sin by grace, which indeed depended on, and originated in, faith and Christ the head." Other saints need to be saved from both guilt and pain. The grace given to Mary takes away guilt, but not pain. Remaining subject to the pain which results from "the evil of the flesh" (*carnis foeditas*), the Virgin was "freed by Christ from original sin, though in another way than others. Others were raised after falling; the Virgin was, as it were, supported in the fall itself so that she would not tumble. . . ." In this case, the objections (a-f) do not prove that "the blessed Virgin had the infection of original sin in its effects, but only in its cause." I take it that, in this view, Mary was not exempt from the bodily pains of the common human condition, though she was freed from original guilt. The word sin (*peccatum*) is used ambiguously, as it designates guilt alone or both guilt and pain.

This is not, however, Bonaventure's own position. He now presents the opinion of "others," with whom he is going to agree. For them, "the Virgin's sanctification followed her contracting original sin; and this, because no one but only the Son of the Virgin was exempt from the guilt of original sin," in keeping with Rom 3:23, supported by the gloss and Augustine (*Tract in* Jn 31:5).

If this presentation may seem excessively condensed, Bonaventure explains at length that this doctrine is "more common, more reasonable, and safer."

First, it is more common. "Nearly all" hold that Mary had original sin, as is suggested by the many sufferings of her life. One must not believe that her sufferings served "for the redemption of others"; nor may one say that they were freely chosen (*per assumptionem*); rather, they were "contracted" (*per contractionem*), that is, induced by original sin in Mary.

Second, this position is more reasonable because "*esse* precedes *bene esse*": to be united to flesh pertains to the soul's *esse*; to have divine grace is of its *bene esse*.[6] With her soul's natural being there came "the infection of original sin" before Mary was sanctified.

Third, this opinion is safer. For it tallies with "the authority of the saints," who repeat what Paul said in Rom 5:12. Bonaventure then reminisces about his theological studies in Paris: "Not one of those we have heard with our own ears has been found to say that the Virgin Mary was exempt from original sin." These are undoubtedly the theologians of the early Franciscan school: Alexander of Hales (d. 1245), Jean de la Rochelle, master-regent (d. 1245), Eudes Rigault (d. 1275), who was master-regent from 1245 to 1247, when he became archbishop of Rouen, and probably several others. Moreover, this view respects "the piety of faith," according to which, "even though the Mother should be held in reverence and one should have great devotion toward her, nonetheless one should have much greater devotion toward the Son, from whom all her honor and glory come." Because "Christ is the Redeemer and Savior of all," who opened the gate to all and who died for all, "in no way should the Virgin be excluded from this universality, lest, while the Mother's excellence is increased, the Son's glory be diminished; and thus the Mother would be provoked, who wants her Son to be more extolled and honored than herself, the Creator more than the creature."

The conclusion is unequivocal:

> Adhering therefore to this position for the honor of Jesus Christ, which in no way mitigates the Mother's honor since the Son incomparably surpasses the Mother, we hold, in keeping with the common opinion, that the Virgin's sanctification took place after she had contracted original sin.

The answers to objections bring no additional material. Yet two of them deserve mentioning. In ad 4, Bonaventure, although he is always attentive to esthetic suggestions, objects that it would be absurd to posit, in the Virgin's case, a cause without its effects. . . . Ad 3 is of greater import. Even if Mary's honor is referred to her Son, it does not follow that all the honor given the Son should also be given the Mother. "And because this honor—that is, to be exempt from all sin, original as well as actual—belongs only to the Son of God, because he alone was conceived of the Holy Spirit and born of a virgin, it should not be ascribed to the Virgin." The other dignities that she has received from her Son, "by which she surpasses all human praises and devotions, are enough for her. And therefore it is not opportune to invent new honors for the Virgin who has no need of our lie, who is filled only with the truth."

To complete his position, Bonaventure, in q. 3, endorses the belief that the Virgin was sanctified before her birth. His main reason is liturgical: "The whole church celebrates her nativity, which it would not do unless she had been sanctified." As to the day or the hour, no one knows; yet the infusion of grace probably followed the infusion of her soul immediately. "This is not expressly in Scripture," yet it finds support in both the Old and the New Testaments. That Scripture should not speak of it is normal, since "the Gospels begin with John, who was the consummation of the prophets and the beginning of the new law," and the Virgin was born before John. Yet the New Testament mentions the sanctification of John in the womb, and the Old that of Jeremiah. The Virgin's holiness, however, was greater than theirs. They were sanctified because of their nearness to Christ, Jeremiah by prophecy (see Jer 32:22, which says more than Is 7:14) and John as his immediate herald. Bonaventure rules out sanctification in the womb in the case of Job (see Jb 1:29, 36), Jacob, and David, as this has "neither certainty nor clear authority, unless someone wants to do violence to Scripture." At any rate, one may properly conclude from the sanctification of Jeremiah and John to that of the Virgin, as she is so much greater than they.

* * * * *

What resulted from Mary's sanctification in the womb?

This is the topic of a. 2. Bonaventure sees no difficulty in admitting that Mary was then freed from all sin, original and actual:

> Because the blessed Virgin Mary is the advocate of sinners, the glory and crown of the just, the banquet-hall (*triclinium*) of the entire Trinity and especially the resting-place (*reclinatorium*) of the Son, it follows that by a special grace of God sin found no room in her" (q. 1).

Yet it is puzzling that he not only argues from congruity, but also alludes to some vague private revelation: "I have heard it narrated that she revealed to some person that her heart never did reprehend her during her whole life."

Problems arise, however, when one tries to figure out whether all concupiscence was also extinguished in Mary by her pre-natal sanctification. Here a distinction is introduced between a first and a second sanctification, that is, between the effect on Mary's holiness of her pre-natal purification and of the Annunciation. In q. 2, Bonaventure determines that in her first sanctification Mary was affected by "such a grace of perfection" that the concupiscence of her sensuality held no sway over her inclinations (c.). She was indeed "full of grace" to the extent that "was proper for her capacity to merit" (ad 1). This "perfect grace" quieted her "soul and faculties" (ad 2-3). The root of concupiscence remained, but in such a reduced state that the resulting leanings were "completely weakened" (ad 4). This position mediates between two others, one of which denies all extinction of concupiscence at any time in Mary, the other holding that all concupiscence was taken away from her twice in

different ways. The first opinion, however, disregards
the ties between the flesh of Christ and that of his Mother.
The second is, Bonaventure thinks, "difficult to understand . . ." (c.).

As second sanctification, the Annunciation filled Mary
with grace in a new way: beyond sanctifying grace, which
she had already received, she was given a grace of con-
firmation in the good (*gratia in bono confirmans*), and this
for a Christological reason: "She was so united to her
Son that in no way would he permit her to be separated
from himself" (c.). As he often does, Bonaventure points
out the structural beauty that ensues: Christ, "the Holy
of Holies," did not and could not sin; the Virgin Mary
was "liberated from the mass of sin (*massa peccati*)" in
two stages: her first sanctification brought her such holiness that "she had the power and faculty to avoid all
mortal sin, . . . the frequency of venial sins, . . . and even all
sin, both particularly and universally." At this level, she
experienced "the three degrees of sanctification," those
of Jeremiah, of John the Baptist and of herself. Later,
when "she carried the Holy of Holies in her womb,"
she was sanctified "in conformity with her Son." Curiously
enough, Bonaventure illustrates this with the alleged
testimony of Jews: ". . . certain Jews have declared that,
although Mary was very beautiful, she was never desired
by any man" (c.).

Two responses to objections are worth recording. In
ad 2, someone asserts that Mary did experience doubt.
But this, Bonaventure retorts, could not be the doubt
that stems from lack of faith. It was the doubt of the mystics:
"a kind of doubt that comes from immense admiration,"
when "one is overwhelmed and as though thrown out of

oneself by the sight of a wonderful thing." In ad 4, Bonaventure admits that, indeed, in the normal order of things, the incapacity to sin pertains to heaven; "but nothing makes it impossible that, by special grace, what is commonly given in heaven (*in patria*) be granted to someone on the way (*in via*), and above all to the person who, when living on earth, was the queen of those who exult in the heavens" (i.e., of the angels).

Further in his Commentary, when studying the natural defects by which Christ suffered and died, Bonaventure specifies that such defects were in Christ by choice rather than by necessity. He then reviews what happened at the Annunciation:

> The Holy Spirit, coming into the Virgin and making her fecund, purified her flesh from all stain of corruption, but left its passibility. From this flesh the Father's Wisdom, that is, the Son of God himself, built for himself an immaculate body and united this body to himself and to a rational soul, which had immunity from guilt both in itself and in the flesh united to it (d. 15, a. 1, q. 1).

In the Virgin, human passibility—the capacity to suffer—derived from "the crime of original sin as necessarily contracted." Christ's passibility was without any trace of crime, from the sole permissive will of God.

Indeed, in an event like the Passion of her Son, Mary experienced a conflict in her will. In this she was like Christ himself in his humanity, and like the many saints who have also suffered with the sufferings of Christ. In so suffering they have experienced a tension between what Bonaventure calls an absolute will and a conditional will. The first prays that God's will be done; the second desires what is pleasing to the human nature. "In their absolute will they wanted what God willed; yet in their conditional will, or will of piety, they had to want the opposite. In so willing they merited, since it is not only natural but also rational."[7] The expression seems obscure. But the sense appears clearly if we reflect that a merely natural desire, being unfree because influenced by sin, is no source or cause of a reward; the rational will is, by definition, freely chosen, and as such it can be a source of merit. One would of course have to add, in the light of the doctrine of grace, that such a rational meritorious will does not exist apart from the grace which transforms what is merely natural into what is rational.

Mary's holiness provides the background for Bonaventure's approach to her "merit" regarding the coming of Christ. Did she conceive the divine Word by pure grace, or did she also somehow deserve to conceive him? This is discussed in d. 4, a. 2, q. 2.

What is merit? Bonaventure's definitions are simple: in merit *congrui*, a sinner "disposes himself for grace"; in merit *digni*, the just, praying for others, deserve to be heard; in merit *condigni*, one deserves a glory proportional to one's charity. These categories allow Bonaventure to admit the first two kinds of merit in Mary, but not the third. To say that, before the Annunciation, she merited *de congruo* to conceive the Son of God is to say that "because of her extreme purity, humility, and benignity, she was prepared to be made the Mother of God" (c.). One should of course remember at this point that the purity, humility, and benignity were the work of grace in her.

When the angel came, moreover, she merited not only in congruity but even in dignity "to be overshadowed and impregnated by the power of the Most High." This also was a gift. Yet she never merited to conceive the Son of God by way of condignity,

> for this exceeds all merit, and also because it was the foundation of the glorious Virgin's own merit. Whether we say that God became man or that a woman became the Mother of God, each is above the state that is due to a creature; and therefore the one as the other were by benignity and grace.

Thus one may say that Mary merited not only in congruity but also in dignity, since "by the Holy Spirit's abundant grace she was not only prepared (*congrua*) but even worthy (*digna*)."

Bonaventure is thus led to affirm that charity, as divine gift, "has its perfection in Christ and, I believe, also in the Virgin Mary; some say also in the angels. I know, however, about Christ, that he has as much glory as a creature united [to the Word] can receive, and I believe it also of his most sweet Mother."[8] One should of course remember a point which Bonaventure does not stress here, namely, that if each one's capacity has been filled by grace, that of Christ's humanity is infinitely deeper than that of his Mother, since he alone is in hypostatic union with the Word of God.

Theotocos

Whereas the consideration of Mary's merit falls under

the rubric of her holiness, the study of her "cooperation" with God in the process of the Incarnation serves as introduction to the Christological propriety of her traditional title, *Dei Genitrix*, the strict Latin rendering of *Theotocos*. Here, cooperation does not evoke, with Bonaventure, as it presumably would with most contemporary theologians, Mary's acceptance of the angel's message. It designates only her physical or physiological contribution to the process of the conception and gestation of Jesus. His answer to this preliminary question will enable Bonaventure to take sides on the matter of the title, *Theotocos*.

D. 4, a. 3: "The conception of Christ as related to the Virgin who conceived," is subdivided in three questions:

q. 1: "Whether the Virgin Mary, in this conception, cooperated in something with the Holy Spirit."

q. 2: "Whether this cooperation of the blessed Virgin was natural or miraculous."

q. 3: "Whether the blessed Virgin should be called *Dei Genitrix*."

Q. 1 receives the longest treatment. Bonaventure has no difficulty with the affirmative answer:

> There is no doubt that, since the Virgin Mary is the mother of Christ and is truly said to have conceived him, she truly cooperated in the conception of her Son. The doctors of theology commonly and generally hold this position. But they diverge as to the mode of this cooperation.

Here as elsewhere, agreement on the *that* does not amount to agreement on the *how*. Here, too, one can see the scholastic mind at work, at a time when the growth of a rudimentary technology in the developing cities focused attention on how to do things.

Bonaventure analyzes three options. In the first, Mary cooperated by providing the "material principle" necessary to conception. This is in line with Aristotle's contention (*De gener. anim.*, I, ch. 2) that the female of the species simply presents an unformed matter to be formed by the male through sexual conjunction. Thus the Virgin offered unformed matter, while "the Holy Spirit supplied what was missing from a male." Hence she is properly called mother. This opinion is of course closely related to the view that woman's contribution to the conception of her child is merely passive. On this precise point, however, Bonaventure did not follow Aristotle. From his main source, the *Summa Alexandri,*[9] he had inherited a tradition which, through Avicenna, derived from ancient medical science as known through Hippocrates and Galenus: woman does actively participate in a child's conception. Accordingly, "this position says too little."

Another option would recognize that Mary, who provided indeed the material principle, also cooperated with the Holy Spirit "in the induction of the final form." She could not cooperate in "the instantaneous formation of the body," for this requires God's infinite power. But the instantaneous induction of a final form is a task of nature. "And therefore the Virgin's generative power cooperated with the Holy Spirit in what it could do, and she is called mother in that she effected the conception both in its beginning and in its consummation." One should remember here that the Augustinian scholastic tradition generally held to the theory of a multitude of forms: matter receives several forms until the highest caps them all. The troubles of Thomas Aquinas during the Averroistic controversy will come in part from his denial of the plurality of forms. Yet Bonaventure, despite his acceptance of a plurality of forms, rejects this option. It "says too much." Firstly, it is not consistent. If the conception itself, being an instantaneous formation, results from "uncreated power," then correlatively Jesus was conceived, not from the Virgin, but from the same uncreated power. Secondly, "it does not seem right that the Holy Spirit did the preparation alone and brought about the consummation with the Virgin's cooperation." Thirdly, it is difficult to identify the "final form" in question. For it can be neither Jesus's soul, which is directly created, nor "the bodily organization," which in nature is not instantaneous but progressive.

Having rejected two extremes, Bonaventure finds himself "led in the way of truth." The chief basis for his argument is provided by the previous determination (d. 2, a. 3, q. 2) that, unlike other human bodies, the body of Jesus was formed in the Virgin's womb all at once rather than progressively: "In the first instant of conception the body was brought to the perfection of its organization." The divine power acted in an unusual and wonderful way, for "this is the miracle of miracles, that a woman should conceive God. And therefore, to show his marvelous power, God formed this body instantaneously, which nature cannot form except progressively." Furthermore, Mary was filled with the Holy Spirit and "made the Mother of God as soon as she consented to the angel's message." But it was not proper that God should unite himself with a human body that was not perfect. On the ground of this previous conclusion Bonaventure now asserts that Mary's pregnancy was unique insofar as "God by his power accelerated what in other women is led successively to being." But this implies that Mary received from God the capacity to present a matter that was properly prepared for such a perfect production of her offspring. This matter was not merely passive; it was also sufficient for such a "complete action." Since Jesus's entire human substance was from Mary, she was "the mother of Christ in a truer mode than any woman is the mother of her son." In this way indeed she cooperated with God in the formation of her Son. And for this reason the Scripture says, not only that Christ was *born* of the Virgin (Mt 1:16), but also that he was *"made* from a woman" (Gal 4:4).

The ad 2 of q. 1 contains a notable warning against too much curiosity in such an area:

> Whether the Virgin, actuated by the Holy Spirit, ovulated, that is, emitted semen as a mother does, although some have said it, one should not frequently meditate on such a word, since it is connected with turpitude and one must have pure lips in such a matter, and also since there is no certainty in this and it does not seem to be much in keeping with the words of the saints. Hence it is stupid (*stultum*) in such things thus to want to speculate with curiosity about details. Let it suffice to say that the Virgin provided a matter that was apt to the generation of the Son of God according to the flesh.

In q. 2, Bonaventure explains that Mary's cooperation with the Holy Spirit in the conception of her Son was both natural and miraculous. It was natural, in that being a woman, she functioned "as is proper to the female sex." It was also miraculous, since "the generative power in the Virgin was both actuated by the Holy Spirit and elevated above its capacity." This "capacity above nature" she received at her sanctification. Thus Mary had two generative capacities: "above nature and according to nature," the one given her at her creation, the other at her sanctification. At the Annunciation, that is, "at the moment of conception," both capacities were "constituted in complement of her process of operation." In this way, Mary's cooperation was natural, yet also above nature. To conceive without a man was "admirable and unusual." It was "much above nature, even very much above nature, since this was chiefly marvelous above all marvels, that her virginal womb was at the same time unbroken and fecund." This point is confirmed in ad 3: "There was a double miracle: in the gift of the power to act, and in the act itself." In the case of Sara and Elizabeth, who, though sterile, conceived a son, a miracle removed their sterility. "This, however, was singularly admirable, that neither the Virgin Mary's fecundity removed her virginity, nor her virginity excluded fecundity."

The Virgin's cooperation in the conception and birth of Christ constitutes the basis for the appellation *Dei Genitrix*. As q. 3 specifies, "the words that express the Christian faith must be far from error and near to devotion, especially those of which the Virgin Mary is the subject." Why devotion? Because "she herself destroyed all heresies in the whole world by conceiving and begetting the Truth; she herself deserved [*promeruit*, in the sense explained in d. 4, a. 2, q. 2] reconciliation for the whole humankind; and therefore all the devotion of Christians should be burning toward her." As the one she conceived must be called "not only Christ after the union but also true God on account of the eternal generation," she should be called *Dei Genitrix*. Thus is she honored and Nestorius's error is stifled. It is "justly, truly, and devotedly that the blessed Virgin is to be called *Dei Genitrix*" (c.). Indeed she is also *"Christotocos"* (ad 4); yet this expression ought to be shunned since Nestorius hid his venom in it (c.). That the Virgin was in no way "consubstantial" with her Son according to the divine nature is not a valid objection. She is not called "Mother of God because she would have begotten him according to the divine nature, but because of the communication of idioms, the expression of the mystery of the Incarnation, and the honor of the Virgin herself" (ad 2).

The divine motherhood is thus closely connected with the virginity of Mary, who remained a virgin in view of it.

Virginity

Discussing the nature of matrimony in the treatise on the sacraments which forms book IV of the Commentary, Bonaventure faces again the question whether matrimony necessarily implies a mutual consent to sexual union (d. 28, a. un., q. 6). Most of the discussion hinges on Mary's matrimonial consent. Four positions are listed, the last having the author's favor.

1° Some think that sexual union is of the essence of marriage. Then Mary did consent to it; and she could do so if she had not vowed virginity even though she intended to remain a virgin. But this Bonaventure deems derogatory to Mary. For, without a vow of virginity, she would not be "the Virgin above all virgins."

2° For Honorius of Autun in the *Summa aurea*, matrimonial consent need not be particular and explicit; Mary's consent was only general and implicit. But this, for Bonaventure, is not satisfactory. For Mary was well acquainted with the nature of marriage and she was informed about sexual union. Given this knowledge, she had explicitly to consent or not to consent to it.

3° Others believe that Mary consented to sexual union "if it pleased God." Yet this is insufficient. For every good consent, even when it is formulated absolutely, remains conditionally dependent on God's will: one cannot properly consent to what is against the divine will. This being the case, Mary could not have agreed to sexual union, even conditionally, since she already knew God's will in regard to her virginity.

4° Matrimonial consent gives the spouses the mutual property of their bodies, and this mutual property is expressed differently in consenting to the marriage vows and in consummating the marriage. "Because the blessed Virgin knew by divine inspiration, or perhaps from Joseph himself, that he would never want to use his right over her body but would preserve her virginity, she could and she should commit or give herself to him." She may also have considered making her vow of virginity public, since the Law enforced the keeping of vows even if no one yet had dared to vow virginity. This fourth opinion is that of Bonaventure.

The answers to objections bring no new material. Yet they illustrate the importance, in Bonaventure's theology, of safeguarding what he calls the "piety of faith":

> We cannot deny that there was a true marriage between Mary and Joseph, since this is said in the evangelical Scripture, and all the saints agree. Moreover, the piety of faith and respect for the Virgin do not allow us to think that her most blessed, pure, and whole soul was leaning a little toward the work of the flesh; nor do I believe that she herself entertained any doubt about it (ad 5).

Nonetheless, Bonaventure does not feel too strongly about his own application of this principle to the point in question. He adds: "If, however, someone says otherwise, provided he does not insult the Virgin, one should not make much fuss. For one should diligently strive lest our Lady's honor, which must be totally preserved even in danger of death, be diminished at all by any one."

Discussion of Mary's marriage leads by an easy step to consideration of her virginity, and first of all to her vow. That Mary remained a virgin is not debated. That she had vowed virginity is also generally, though not universally, taken for granted. The critical point, in Bonaventure's eyes, is not whether Mary had vowed her virginity to God, but whether, given this vow, her consent to matrimony was "in itself orderly and honest." This is the topic of IV, d. 30, a un., q. 2. There are some who maintain that Mary, after her vow, should not have been espoused to anyone. Bonaventure admits with them that "first Mary vowed, then she married, and she married this man Joseph." But he opposes to them the principle that "everything in this marriage was done by an intimate counsel of the Holy Spirit." The corpus of his response consists in looking, in the light of this principle, at the three steps of Mary's marriage.

First, Mary vowed virginity. This was done in order that the eternal Wisdom, who is "the refulgence and the spotless mirror of eternal light" (Wis 7:25) could be "conceived by a Mother who was incorruptible both in reality and in a firm will; and perfect incorruption of the will lies in the vow of virginity." A second reason was that she would be "the example of total virginity for women," as Christ would be for men. A third reason was that she would have "the privilege of all nobility and sanctity":

> Far from it that another virgin should surpass the blessed Mary; rather, the "Most High," who "established her" (Ps 85:5), adorned her with the privilege of every dignity, so that, just as he loved her above the others, so she would be holier than the others and lovable to all. Whence, prescinding from her divine motherhood, she must still be loved and praised before the other saints; and therefore the Holy Spirit, who inspired others to vow virginity, did not keep it secret from her.

Second, Mary married. This in turn was proper. For it was a sign of the nuptiality of the Church, which is "spiritual bride and virgin and mother." The virgin and mother who signified this had evidently to be married. This would also protect her from infamy. And it would hide the divine purpose from the devil.

Third, Mary married this particular man, on account of his tribe (Juda) and lineage (David), of his chastity and righteousness and of his poverty, by which "the humility of Christ and of the glorious Virgin is manifested, and the pride of the worldly confounded" (c.).

Should one object that vows of virginity belong to the gospel, whereas Mary lived under the law, Bonaventure would respond: "How was she under the law, who begat the author of the law? Further, if those who are led by the spirit of God (Rom 8:14) are not under the law, she who was filled with the Holy Spirit did not belong to the law but to the gospel, which God's finger, the Holy Spirit, had written in her heart from her infancy" (ad 1-2).

The virginity of Mary is constantly assumed by Bonaventure. The Christological doctrine that she must be called *Theotocos* has been identified as the locus for the belief in her virginity. We are brought back to the topic, still in a Christological setting, in III, d. 12, a. 3, q. 2, when Bonaventure studies the humanity of Christ: "Whether Christ should have assumed flesh from both a man and a woman rather than from a woman alone."

The solution affirms the divine power: the Incarnation could have been from the two sexes or from one alone (either one). God could have purified the generative power of a man just as he did that of the Virgin. It follows that the reasons for Mary's virginity belong to congruence, not to necessity. Four are proposed: first, the Mother's dignity, for she "did not lose the privilege of virginity by reason of the conception of the Son of God"; second, the Father's honor, for it would have been injurious to "the first Father" in heaven if Christ had had a second father on earth, as then he would not have been fully the son of either; third, the (esthetic) perfection of the universe, so that there would be four ways of bringing a human being into the world: from man and woman, from neither man nor woman (Adam), from man alone (Eve), from woman alone (Jesus); fourth, the "correspondence of congruity between the fall and the restoration": as the fall, begun with Eve, was completed in Adam, so in the restoration "a woman by believing and conceiving began in a hidden way to triumph over the devil, and afterwards her Son in the open conquered him in battle—on the gibet of the cross." This last reason clearly assumes a notion of recapitulation in the sense of St Irenaeus.[10]

In another perspective, which is both Christological and Trinitarian, Bonaventure throws light on the nature of the virginal conception. How did the Virgin conceive? It was a fruit of love. "What most of all prepared the Virgin for the conception of the Son of God was divine love" (d. 4, a. 1, q. 1). Bonaventure suggests a bold parallel between normal bi-sexual conception and that of Christ. It is not that the Holy Spirit became Mary's husband, but that love is the principle of both kinds of conception. Ordinarily, "a woman conceives through a man's love and union with him, which takes place with desire and love for the generative power." In the Incarnation, "the blessed Virgin singularly conceived from God by the singularity of her love." Divine *caritas* being appropriated to the Spirit, she is said to have conceived from the Holy Spirit. Indeed, "the Incarnation manifested the divine power, wisdom, and goodness," three attributes that are "most excellently and principally appropriated to the three Persons." Christ's virginal conception could be attributed to each of the three Persons. Yet, given the centrality of love in the process leading to conception, the appropriation of it to the Holy Spirit has the preference of

Scripture: the Virgin conceived *de Spiritu Sancto*.

* * * * *

"Neither the blessed Virgin nor Christ [in his humanity] surpasses the angels by reason only of their nature, but [they so do] by reason of their manifold grace."[11] This is the high point of Bonaventure's perspective on Mary. She has been raised above the angels. Bonaventure in fact develops an elaborate angelology as part of his doctrine on creation. He holds pronounced views on the angels' role as agents of the divine glory and servants of the Word, on the angelic organization or hierarchy, which functions as a heavenly model for the structure of the Church on earth.[12] Mary's elevation above the angels is justified by her task as the Forthbringer of God. It is, as it were, a major side effect of her being called, and being by grace enabled to accept, to become the Mother of the Word made flesh. Thus the epic of Mary, which started with the humble beginnings of an ordinary girl from Galilee, climaxed above the angels in the heavenly realm. There, one cannot say that the epic has ended, since Mary is now living, along with all the saints of the church triumphant, in the divine glory. This epic is described symbolically at the very beginning of the Commentary on the Sentences, in the prologue which introduces the reader to the aridity of the four books, with their monotonous sequence of distinctions, articles, and questions. Bonaventure proposes the basic "metaphor" of the four rivers flowing from paradise. The first river is the eternal emanation of the divine Persons. The second is the creation of the universe and all it contains. The third is the Incarnation of the Son of God, by which what has flowed from God flows back to the source. The fourth is the dispensation of the sacraments. . . . The third river is, for the faithful, the only way to the Father, from whom it proceeds at its origin. Secondarily, however, it may also be seen in relation to the mother from whom the Son also comes:

> To this river as to his origin from the mother one may apply what is said in Mardochai's dream (Est 10:6): *A small rivulet has grown into a river, and it has been changed into light and sun.* Who, may I ask, is this small rivulet but the most humble Virgin? She grew into a river when she begat Christ, who is not only river by abundance of grace, but is also called Light of wisdom and Sun of justice, according to what John says of him: *He was the true Light . . .* (Jn 1:9).[13]

Notes

1. The following quotations are from C.S., I, prologue, q. 1. See my study, *Transiency and Permanence. The Method of Theology according to St Bonaventure,* (St Bonaventure: Franciscan Institute, 1954) (repr., 1974).

2. These references are to book III, where Christological questions are studied. In order to simplify footnotes, I will not give references specifically for each quotation. Where the reference is provided in the main text, I will not add it in a footnote; and one reference will cover all quotations until the next one.

3. This is precisely the area where the older theology differed from that of John Duns Scotus. The problem of Mary's conception was brought up, as we shall see, by the spread of a liturgical feast, originally unauthorized, of her conception. Bernard, Bonaventure, and Thomas Aquinas argued against the legitimacy of the feast.

4. The "revelation" alluded to here is no more than a medieval legend. Helsin, abbot of the monastery of Ramsay, England, sent to Denmark on an embassy by king William the Conqueror, ran into a heavy storm on the North Sea. Fearing for his life, he prayed to the Virgin. According to the legend, he then received a vision: a "venerable pontiff" appeared to him and told him that he would be saved from drowning if he promised to celebrate the Conception of the Virgin on December 8, and to spread the devotion through his preaching. The legend was taken seriously, in part because it was contained in a writing that was (wrongly) attributed to St Anselm of Canterbury, the *Epistola venerabilis Anselmi ad coëpiscopos Angliae ad Conceptionem celebrandam.*

5. Mary's Assumption is not examined directly in the Commentary. See below, chap. 8. Unlike the definition of 1950, the medieval tradition assumed that Mary died before being assumed to heaven, a point which is not denied, yet is not included, in Pius XII's dogmatic definition.

6. One may note that the distinction between "plain existence" (*esse*) and "good existence" (*bene esse*) is not original to Anglican theology, in which it has been widely used in debates over episcopacy (does it belong to the *esse* or to the *bene esse* of the Church?). *Esse*, however, in the medieval language, means "existence" rather than "essence."

7. I, d. 48, a. 2, q. 2, ad 4.

8. I, d. 17, a. un., q. 4.

9. The *Summa Alexandri*, which presents the teaching of the earlier Franciscan school, was largely the work of Alexander's followers and colleagues, chiefly of Jean de la Rochelle. On Bonaventure's theology of womanhood, see Emma Thérèse Healy, *Woman according to Saint Bonaventure*, (Erie, Pa: Villa Maria College, 1956).

10. See below, chapter X.

11. II, d. 1, p. 2, a. 2, q. 2, ad 3.

12. I have described Bonaventure's angelology in my volume, *Die Engel* (*Handbuch der Dogmengeschichte*, II, 2b), (Freiburg: Herder, 1968), 68-70 (French tr.: *Les Anges*, Paris: Le Cerf, 1971, 168-174; Spanish tr.: *Los Angeles*, Madrid: BAC, 1973, p. 63-66).

13. I, prologue, 3°.

CHAPTER 3

A FIRST SYNTHESIS

So far in our research, Bonaventure has focussed attention on specific questions regarding the Virgin Mary. He has done so with soft, occasional touches in his early *dubia circa litteram*. He has done so more earnestly and more thoroughly in the Commentary on the Sentences. Most theological questions that may be asked concerning Mary's ties to Christ have been treated at more or less greater length. The only important point of more recent Marian doctrine that does not seem to have been examined is the problem of Mary's being assumed into heaven at the end of her earthly life. Mary's Assumption will in reality figure prominently in Bonaventure's sermons. But it holds no major place, in fact hardly any place at all, at the level of his systematic theology as formulated in the Commentary on the Sentences. The corresponding doctrine was already in quiet possession in the Catholic Church. It was of course, at the time, a point of piety rather than of formal theology since it had not yet been formulated officially in any definitive way. Admittedly, Mariology as such did not figure in the Commentary as a specific topic: it was Christology which brought about discussion of Mary. The dominant point of view was that of her title and function as *Dei Genitrix*, the Forthbringer of God.

This was already the central point of what the *dubia* had to say about the holy Virgin. Yet the title which appears the most often in these is *Mater Dei*, the Mother of God. It is presumably significant that Bonaventure switched to *Dei Genitrix* in his more systematic investigations. Although the two expressions may be translated as "Mother of God," the connotations differ. *Mater Dei* conveys a more static vision of the Virgin-Mother, corresponding to the statue of Mary without the child. In fact, both romanesque and gothic art favored the statue, painting, or window showing Mary holding the child. Yet the representation of the Virgin standing by herself as though facing God or, in some cases, facing the people at prayer, is not unknown in medieval art, even though it is not found there as often as it will be in the baroque art of the Counter-Reformation. At any rate, *Dei Genitrix* connotes a more dynamic relationship between Mary and the divine child: she is the one who receives him as the Uncreated Word and brings him forth as the Incarnate Word. Precisely, these are two of the three basic categories of Bonaventure's Christology. The third refers to the Inspired (or, as I would prefer to say, the In-Spirited) Word, that is, the Word present and active in the heart of the faithful and in humanity as a whole through the Holy Spirit. In this perspective, the Annunciation is, for the Virgin, the focal point where these three dimensions of the Word have become one: for it was by the over-shadowing of the Holy Spirit, that is, through the In-Spirited Word, that the Virgin received the Uncreated Word in order to conceive him as the Incarnate Word. Thus does the Annunciation offer a unique point of view from which one can build a theological synthesis on the Virgin Mary, the Forthbringer of God.

* * * * *

A theological synthesis hinges around a central principle that has been carefully chosen. It was precisely around the Annunciation that Bonaventure built his first theological synthesis on Mary. One finds it in the *Breviloquium,* part 4, chapter 3. A word about this short work and its method will help understand the Marian synthesis that is contained in it.

This relatively small book—as compared with the Commentary—was explicitly written for the purpose of helping the students or readers who frequently feel lost in the Commentaries on the Sentences, in the writings of the church Fathers, and even in the holy Scripture itself "as in a dark forest."[1] In order to do this, Bonaventure selected the highest and therefore the most embracing principle he could find. Theology, as he himself states, "treats of God and of the first principle, since, being the highest knowledge and doctrine, it resolves all things into God as their first and highest principle...."[2] Indeed, one cannot possibly think of a higher and more primordial principle than God, the Creator. Bonaventure therefore tries to determine, for each of the seven mysteries he studies in this book, how this mystery relates to God as to its highest and primordial principle. These mysteries are: 1° "The Trinity of God," 2° "the creature of the world," 3° "the corruption of sin," 4° "the Incarnation of the Word," 5° "the grace of the Holy Spirit," 6° "the sacramental medicine," 7° "the state of the final judgment."

The highest principle of the Incarnation of the Word can be no other than God the Father. For the Incarnation is determined by its purpose, which is the "reparation" of the created world, damaged by human sin. Repairs belong to the *bene esse* of reality, the welfare of the universe; but welfare, "good existence" (*bene esse*) is of no less value than existence (*esse*), than the existence of what was created by God in the first instance:

> To repair creaturely things is no less than to bring them into existence, just as to exist well is no less than simply to exist. Hence it was therefore most fitting that the principle of reparation be the supreme God, so that, as God created all things through the Uncreated Word, he would heal all things through the Incarnate Word.[3]

Bonaventure will present the Incarnation in three chapters which discuss "the union of natures, the fulness of charisms, and the courage of the sufferings"[4] born for the redemption of humankind. In turn, the union of natures—which is, in philosophical terms, the Incarnation of the divine Word as a man—will be seen from three points of view: *opus, modus, tempus,* namely, its essence (what it is), its mode (how it took place), and its moment (when it was effected).[5] At the level of the mode the Virgin Mary is brought into the discussion. This ties up

remarkably well, as was suggested above, with the primacy
of the Annunciation. Mary properly belongs within the
mystery of the Incarnation, being essentially related
to its mode:

> Concerning the mode of the Incarnation one must
> hold that, when the angel announced to the most
> blessed Virgin Mary that the mystery of the Incarna-
> tion would be fulfilled in her, the Virgin believed,
> desired, and consented; the Holy Spirit came into
> her to sanctify and fecund her, and by his power
> "the Virgin conceived the Son of God, whom the
> Virgin begat, and after begetting she remained a
> Virgin."[6]

Such is, in the *Breviloquium*, Bonaventure's formulation
of faith insofar as it includes the Virgin Mary. It remains
to understand it, in the Bonaventurian sense of the word:
to understand a point of faith is to place it in its proper
setting in relation to other points of faith, to Scripture,
the tradition, the requirements of piety, reason, and
spiritual esthetics. In the general pattern of the *Breviloquium*,
each chapter, beginning with the statement of faith, continues with a series of reasons in support of this statement.
These reasons come in the form of a triplet, each item
of which relates the formula of faith to its first principle
in God: "The Incarnation is an action (*opus*) which proceeds from the first principle, insofar as this principle
heals in a mode that is most congruous, most universal
and most complete."[7] Its congruity points to divine
wisdom, its universality to divine liberality, its perfection
to divine power. These three aspects of the mode of the

Incarnation, imaging three major attributes of God, are then taken up one by one.

The congruity of the mode of the Incarnation emerges from the principle, already at work in both the *dubia* and the Commentary, of recapitulation. It is proper "that the medicine correspond by opposition to the disease, the restoration to the fall, and the remedy to the epidemic."[8] There follows a contrasted parallel between the doing of Eve and the task of the Virgin:

> Since humankind fell by diabolical suggestion, by the consent of a deceived woman, and by the libidinous generation which transmits original sin to offsprings, it was opportune that, on the contrary, there would be here [at the Annunciation] a good angel inciting to good, and a Virgin believing and consenting to the suggested good, and the love of the Holy Spirit sanctifying and fecundating her for an immaculate offspring (*conceptum*) so that in this way 'contraries be healed by contraries.'

In keeping with the principle of the redeeming balance of contraries, the Virgin Mary was "the woman who, taught by the angel, sanctified and fecundated through the Holy Spirit, without any corruption of mind or of body, begat the child who would give grace, holiness, and life to all who would come to him." Thus, congruity, the first aspect of the mode of the Incarnation, shows the divine wisdom at work. The Annunciation balances the fall of humanity in Eve by bringing to Mary, with her consent, the healer of the human race. Congruity reveals the design of God in its cosmic scope. The unfortunate beginnings of humanity will be counter-balanced, at the fulness of time (*tempus*), by Mary's *fiat*, her acceptance of a new mode of being, the mode of faith.

In its universal dimension, the mode of the Incarnation places the Annunciation at the center of a cosmic drama. The fall was a multiple affair: it involved angels and men, heavenly and earthly creatures; in humanity it implied, through Adam and Eve, the two sexes. Thus was the universality of creation tied together in a partnership of sin. Since both humanity, through its first representatives, and a sizable number of the angels had fallen, the remedy that was to restore creation to God's good purpose needed the character of totality; it had to be universal in scope so as to reach all who were sick. Hence the three actors of the Annunciation, who themselves pre-supposed the involvement of the three divine Persons:

> It was most proper that an angel, a woman and a man contribute to the mystery of the Incarnation: the angel as the herald, the virgin woman as conceiving, the man as the conceived offspring, so that the angel Gabriel would be the eternal Father's messenger, the immaculate Virgin would be the temple of the Holy Spirit, the conceived offspring would be the Person itself of the Word.[9]

The notion of "hierarchy" comes in at this point. It is of major importance in Bonaventure's esthetic outlook on the universe. "Hierarchy," a traditional term inherited from the spiritual and theological writings attributed to "Denys the Areopagite," designates for Bonaventure an analogical correspondence between the divine Trinity, the heavenly realm of the church triumphant (which comprises the angels and the saints), and the church militant here on earth. Within this correspondence it also implies a scale of dignity, which can be seen, according to the point of view, as descending like cascading lights from above, or as ascending, like the return of sinful humanity to reunion with its Creator. When looked at by Bonaventure in this hierarchic perspective, the Annunciation shows a convergence of the "threefold hierarchy: divine, angelic, and human." To those who understand it, it reveals "the Trinity of God," and "the universality of the good [obtained through the Annunciation], and the liberality of the supreme healer." The common language of Christians speaks of the Holy Spirit as the active divine principle in the Annunciation. Bonaventure at this point introduces the theology of "appropriations," derived from St Augustine: since the works of God are performed by all three Persons in virtue of their common nature, the customary language which attributes some actions to each Person is only a manner of speaking, an appropriation, even though it is grounded in biblical and traditional imagery. "Since liberality and the sanctification of the Virgin in which the conception of the Word was effected are appropriated to the Holy Spirit, it follows that, while the action was done by the entire Trinity, it is said by appropriation that the Virgin conceived from the Holy Spirit." In other words, the universal character of the Annunciation extends to the Virgin's union with God. Through the divine message and her *fiat*, she was united to the action of the Holy Spirit, which was that of the whole Trinity.

* * * * *

Finally, the mode of the Incarnation, as it reflected the first principle which is God, was most complete. And this completion or perfection was effective (going backwards from the outcome to the process and then to the origin) in the offspring, in the conception as such and in the power by which the Virgin conceived.

In the child who was the divine Word made flesh, God's action was supremely and immediately perfect: "At the instant of conception there was not only the forming of the germ, but also its strengthening, its shaping, its vivification by the soul and its deification by the deity united to it."[10] Accordingly, the Virgin "truly conceived the Son of God," and this by virtue of the union of her flesh with the deity, by means of her rational soul acting as congruous medium to prepare her flesh adequately for this union.

In regard to the conception itself, the perfection of the process may be seen in the point already made by Bonaventure in the Commentary on the Sentences: there are four ways, and no more, to bring someone into the world, the ways of Adam (from neither man nor woman), of Eve (from man alone), of ordinary humans (from both a man and a woman), and finally that which is unique to Christ, from a woman alone, the Virgin Mary. Thus the Annunciation put as it were the keystone to the perfection of the universe.

As to the divine power in virtue of which the Incarnation took place, Bonaventure sees it in the threefold action of innate, infused, and uncreated power. The innate capacity of the Virgin provided the basic material from her own flesh. The infused power of the Holy Spirit sanctified her as was appropriate. The uncreated power immediately brought the process to perfection, thus doing in one instant what created power can only do step by step. Hence Bonaventure's conclusion, which, as in the Commentary, brings together the divine power of the Holy Spirit and the immensity of the Virgin's love for God:

> And thus the most blessed Virgin Mary was mother in the most complete way possible, as she conceived the Son of God without a man, by the Holy Spirit's fecundation. Because the Holy Spirit's love was burning singularly in the Virgin's soul, the Holy Spirit's power wrought marvels in her flesh, as grace excited, assisted, and lifted up her nature as was required for this admirable conception.

Notes

1. Brev., prol., 6, n. 5. I have used the text of this work in the Spanish edition, *Obras de San Buenaventura*, vol. I, (Madrid: BAC, 1945).

2. l. c., n. 6.

3. Brev., p. 4, ch. 1, n. 2.

4. These topics are respectively covered in ch. 2-4; 5-6; 7.

5. These aspects of the Incarnation are covered in ch. 2, 3, and 4.

6. Brev., IV, ch. 3, n. 1.

7. Ch. 3, n. 2.

8. Ch. 3, n. 3.

9. Ch. 3, n. 4.

10. Ch. 3, n. 5.

Part Two

Scriptural Meditation

CHAPTER 4

MARY IN
ST LUKE'S GOSPEL

The Seraphic Doctor is known to posterity chiefly as a theologian and as a mystic and spiritual author, not as a biblical exegete. Yet commenting on the Bible was an integral part of the task of a professor of theology in a medieval university. The professor in fact commented on Scripture twice in his career: first, rapidly (*cursorie*), to provide an initiation to biblical literature, and, later, more elaborately for the determination of theological questions. This itself took two main forms: the professor presided at, and finalized the text of, theological disputations; and he also commented doctrinally and at length on specific books of the Scriptures. Besides his better known Commentary on the Sentences, Bonaventure himself left both several "disputed questions" and some commentaries on a few biblical books, namely, on *Ecclesiastes* (though the authenticity of it has been doubted) and the *Book of Wisdom* for the Old Testament, on the Gospels of St Luke and St John for the New. How important was

Scripture in his eyes clearly appears from his prologue to the *Breviloquium*, in which Bonaventure measures the "breadth," the "length," the "height" and the "depth" of Scripture, that is, the multitude of its parts, its description of times and ages, its description of the ordered hierarchies of the universe and the Church, and the multitude of its mystical senses and meanings.

It is generally agreed that Bonaventure must have lectured on the Bible between 1248 and 1250, when he was only a "biblical bachelor," and that the present form of his commentaries is slightly more recent, having been touched up or rewritten by himself after 1252. As regards the New Testament, the *Commentary on Luke*, although it was most probably delivered first, is in fact the most finished. The *Commentary on John*, while it is much more succinct, exists in two forms: the more basic one is a brief survey of the Gospel, most probably along the lines of what was expected from the young instructor who gave students their first initiation to the biblical text. The second, called *Collationes* or Sermons, is in the form of a series of notes and outlines for homilies on selected themes in the Gospel of John.[1]

In the present chapter we will look at the Gospel of Luke, the less elaborate Marian passages of the other commentaries being left for the next chapter.

* * * * *

Bonaventure must have been greatly impressed by Aristotle's theory of the four causes as it was used in the rhetoric of his time. He introduced the *Commentary on the Sentences* with a lengthy prologue on the fourfold

causality of the book of Sentences. He also introduced
each of his four biblical commentaries with an investigation of their four causes. Two causes—efficient and final—
are extrinsic. Two—formal and material—are intrinsic to
the book. The efficient cause of the Gospel of Luke is itself
threefold: the highest is the Spirit of the Lord; the lowest
is Luke himself; the intermediate is "the unction of grace,"
which "disposed his soul to receive the texts of the truth
from the greatest Doctor."[2] The final cause, which is also
threefold, is the "manifestation of truth," the "healing of
our sickness," the "opening of eternity." The material
cause is no other than the topic of the Gospel: this is
"Christ, as mediator, preacher, redeemer and victor."
The entire Gospel of Luke is therefore Christocentric. It
should be understood and explained in reference to
Christ. The same principle as in Bonaventure's speculative
theology is therefore operative in his biblical commentaries: all that will be touched upon in time will be
dealt with because of its relationship to Christ. Bonaventure, who follows St Jerome's declarations regarding
the meanings of Hebrew names, believes that "Mary"
means, in keeping with Balaam's prophecy (Nm 24:17),
"star of the Sea."[3] This "name is filled with mystery in its
triple interpretation, by which we understand the three
states of those who must be saved: the active by the salted
sea (*mare amarum*), the contemplative by the star, the
prelates by the power (*dominium*)." The very name of
Mary thus evokes the purpose and extent of salvation
by Christ.

Bonaventure's method in commenting on Scripture
does not help contemporary readers to see the broad
lines of his thought. For he comments chiefly through

extensive quotations from the Old and the New Testaments, seeking whatever in the Bible can illustrate, literally or spiritually, the topic at hand. Then the picture of Mary as a young woman of Nazareth who became the mother of the Lord tends to disappear behind a screen of biblical verses which modern readers may not find appropriate. Their connection with Mary is associative rather than strictly typological. Bonaventure's attention has been attracted by similarities in wording between some remote passage of the Old Testament and the text of the *Magnificat*; and he makes as much of it as the exegesis, the spiritual theology and the Marian devotion of his time will allow. But this traditional method, which was still modern when Bonaventure practiced it, has now become generally obsolete. What must have been to the advantage of his thirteen-century readers has in fact turned into a hindrance for the contemporary taste and look.

Moreover, Bonaventure's extensive culling of scriptural quotations and his search for biblical episodes illustrative of the points in hand are enhanced—or, as some may feel, complicated—by similar quoting from the Fathers of the Church and more recent authors, not least from St Bernard, the great singer of Mary in the twelfth century. This quest for "authorities" in the medieval sense of the term was destined to strengthen Bonaventure's theology and interpretations in the eyes of his scholastic readers. It may, indeed, still interest contemporary historians who may wonder about the sources of Bonaventure's thought. Yet it also, unavoidably, acts as an obstacle for the average reader today. With these several handicaps, however, Bonaventure's reflections on Mary in the New Testament may still speak to us, for their theological and Christological depths remain apparent through the successive layers of his exegetical method.

Our chapter will focus on four aspects of Bonaventure's meditative reading of Luke's Gospel: the Annunciation, the Visitation, the absence of Mary in the genealogy, Mary as model of the contemplatives.

The Annunciation

Bonaventure understands the Annunciation on the general model of recapitulation, even if the word does not appear in his explanations. It was proper, as he says after St Bernard and, earlier, after St Irenaeus, that "the reparation correspond to the fall."[4] The Annunciation took place "in the sixth month," that is, in March. This was the month of the creation of the world, and "the reparation had to respond to the first creation." Further, humankind was created on the sixth day, Christ came in the sixth age of the world, in the sixth millenium after creation, in the sixth month, as he was also to suffer on the sixth day of the week (Friday), and to be nailed to the cross at the sixth hour of the day, "so that it be signified that the one who was conceived in the sixth month came at the fulness of time and in perfection."

The angel Gabriel counterbalanced the fallen angel of the temptation of Eve. He came to Nazareth (a word meaning "flower"), a town of Galilee, in the borderland between Jews and Gentiles. "Therefore something good could come from Nazareth, even the flower of all good. It was proper for a flower [the flower of the root of Jesse] to be conceived in a flower, to be nourished in a flower, to be announced at the time of the flowers, which is in the Spring and in March." As the Song of Songs has it, "flowers have appeared in our land."

The Virgin whom the angel visited was "chaste"; yet she also was "tested," since she was engaged to Joseph; and she had been "promised" in the seed of David, to whom both she and Joseph belonged. Her name was called by the angel in order to show that "she had been prepared, and not found by accident":

> What had been shown to Moses in the bush and the flame, to Aaron in the stick and the bloom, to Gideon in the fleece and the dew, Solomon had foreseen in the strong woman and her price, Jeremiah had sung in advance concerning the female and the male, Isaiah had most openly declared regarding the Virgin and the house and at last Gabriel showed in saluting the Virgin herself.

Gabriel, well versed in rhetoric, applied the rule given by Cicero, that an address should have "an introduction, a narration, and a conclusion." The introduction comprises the greeting to the Virgin. This shows her to be "the ark of the covenant," her qualities being suggested by the contents of the ark: she is shown to be "sweet and amiable by manna, venerable by the stick, to be preached about and honored by the divine law." In all this, Mary is "lovable for her beauty," which is the meaning of the angel's word: "Hail, full of beauty," like Esther, who "was very pretty and of incredible beauty, and seen in all eyes as gracious and lovable." Furthermore, Mary's dignity was indicated by the angel's words: "The Lord is with you": thus is she called "queen." She is also praiseworthy, as suggested by her being blessed among women. Bonaventure understands this in three ways: Mary is blessed among women, above women, and by women.

Mary listened, and not only with the ear. Her listening with the ear, "in silence and quiet," showed her in all her modesty. But she also listened with her feelings (*affectu*), in which she was troubled because of the dangers of her virginity. She also listened with her mind, in which she was prudent: "The thoughts of the Virgin, even if they troubled her because of the candor of her innocence, yet did not perturb her owing to the splendor of her intelligence."

In the narration which forms the heart of the angel's address, Gabriel tells her not to fear. In other words, he brings her "joy," because her name has been written in heaven. She has received from God the grace of election, the grace of perfection, and the grace of "espousals, that she may become the bride of God and the mother of the Son." The angel continued with a promise: she will conceive. But this will be a "conception without concupiscence, a birth without parturition and pain"; and this "birth without pain" will be followed by "the fruit of the womb with salvation."

The angel told Mary about her Son's greatness. This will be proportional to his "singular grace, his royal excellence, his eternal power." But Mary does not remain passively in front of the heavenly messenger. She herself, as a "most prudent Virgin," asks questions. She wants to know how this will take place. "For there are three ways of conceiving, one carnal, the second spiritual, and the third admirable and singular. Which will it be?" This had been Nicodemus's question: How can it be? Mary does not ask Zachary's question. For Zachary wanted to know "a way of knowledge, or a sign which would induce faith." Mary, however, is only curious about "the process, so that she may consent." She explains the reason which moves her: "I do not know man; that is, I intend not to know man, and so I am a virgin in mind, in flesh, and in purpose." Bonaventure comments:

> Thus it was not unreasonable to ask how she was to conceive a child, when she did not intend to know man, so that, if it were possible to have both virginity and fecundity, then she would give her consent.

With this query the Virgin deserved a "satisfactory answer," which was duly given by the angel: "To this I respond that you will be fecunded without corruption, you will conceive without concupiscence, you will give birth without pain, because it will not be from male seed but from the power of the Holy Spirit."

As she heard the angel's conclusion, that "all is possible with God," the Virgin was able to formulate her *fiat*, which she did "out of faith": "because in her heart she conceived the word of faith, in her womb she conceived the Son of God." She spoke with humility; and "because the Virgin Mary humbled herself, she prepared herself for grace." Her consent was also "perfected in love": "This is the sweetest voice for men, for angels, and for the Spouse himself," who had wished in the Song of Songs: May your voice resound in my ears, for your voice is sweet and your face beautiful. . . .

Bonaventure's conclusion to this meditative reading of the episode of the Annunciation is worth quoting at length. For it introduces a new consideration into the Marian perspective which his theology has opened and has followed up to this point:

> The angel left her, but the Son of God remained with her; the angel left in appearance, but many angels remained for her protection. . . . These are the most blessed angels, who protected her as the preferred "locus of the divine dwelling"; hence, if they provided the benefit of protection on account of the weakness of the flesh, they gave her a cult of reverence on account of the Mother's dignity, and thus in a way they ascended and descended over her. Whence she was designated by this scale on which the Lord rested and along which the angels descended, as Jacob saw it; and then it follows: "This is no other than the house of God and the gate of heaven," for no one henceforth can enter heaven unless it be through Mary as through the gate. For as God came to us through her, so through her are we to return to God. And therefore she is called house, gate, and scale: *house* for Christ's conception, *gate* for Christ's birth, and *scale* for our ascent to God.

Bonaventure's next lines seem to suggest that he is acquainted with, and presumably himself practices, one of the early forms of the rosary: "Therefore let us not leave her, but, prostrate at her feet, let us always greet her: Hail, full of grace, so that through her who found grace and mercy above all women in the eyes of this great Assuerus, we may find grace and receive mercy at the opportune time."

The Visitation

Bonaventure believes that the "city of Juda," located "in the mountain," to which Mary hastened in order to assist her kinswoman Elizabeth was Jerusalem itself.[5] This has a certain importance in his eyes, since, when Mary entered the house and "saluted" Elizabeth, she not only brought a wish or a word of greeting, she saluted in the etymological sense of *salus*, that is, she "brought salvation" to the holy city by bringing the Savior with her. Elizabeth therefore "heard the word of salvation from the one who had conceived the incarnate Word, in whom alone there is salvation." As the mother was thus "excited," her offspring "rejoiced," leaping in her womb. He rejoiced "in desire," before "the presence of the Savior-Lord," whose forerunner he was. Elizabeth then broke out in words: "Blessed are you among women, and blessed is the fruit of your womb." Thus, as Bonaventure states, confirming what was noted above concerning the rosary, Elizabeth in so saying "completed the angelic greeting." In this completion of the angel's greeting by Elizabeth were the blessings of the most holy women of the Old Testament themselves completed and fulfilled: the blessings of Jahel, of Ruth, of Abigail, of Judith came to fruition in the Mother of the Lord. "Among these women and above these women the Virgin Mary was blessed, for those blessings were fulfilled in her." Elizabeth then proclaimed her surprise and wonder at the coming of the Mother of God to herself, a mere servant. "This is highly praiseworthy and even admirable, that a woman should be the Mother of God (*Mater Dei*), and that the Mother of God should visit a servant of God (*ancillam Dei*)." Mary had the greater dignity of the two. Of her it was written in *Ecclesiasticus*: "I am the mother of beautiful love, of fear, and of holy hope." Accordingly, "because of her maternal dignity the Virgin Mary is to be loved, venerated, and approached with all trust as the mother of the highest mercy." The forerunner praised and blessed the Mother. In Scripture, as Bonaventure remarks, blessings go to the "believers," the "lovers," the "fearful," the "active," the "sufferers" and persecuted, the "contemplative." All these blessings apply to Mary: "For all these reasons the Virgin Mary was blessed, but for a special reason she was most blessed, for she conceived the Son of God." Let us therefore ourselves proclaim:

> Blessed are you, who believed, because by believing you conceived, and by conceiving you brought the plenitude of blessedness to all nations.

Thus the Visitation enhances the place of Mary in a prayer of praise and admiration; she has become a motive for praising God for what she is and what she has done. Yet Mary is not only an occasion for prayer and praise on the part of the faithful. She herself becomes, through her response to Elizabeth, a leader and a model in prayer and praise. Bonaventure follows the song of Mary, her *Magnificat*, verse by verse, looking for literary and contextual precedents and for implications of a theological and spiritual order.

After the prophetic testimony of John the Baptist in the womb, there follows "the song of joy, in which the most blessed Virgin Mary praises the divine clemency for the most excellent grace granted her." Just as "there is no perfect praise unless there be present the proper feeling, the proper motive, and the proper mode," so the Virgin hints at her feeling of praise (*magnificat . . .*), at her motive (*quia respexit . . .*), and at "the scope of the divine praise" (*et misericordia ejus a progenie in progenies . . .*). In her feeling Mary is grateful and humble. For "our soul truly magnifies the Lord when it makes itself captive and humbles itself before him. . . . Whence, the Virgin Mary, because she humbles herself more than others, magnifies the Lord more highly than others." Grateful, Mary is also "joyful, exulting in divine salvation. . . . Because the Virgin Mary sought the Lord and loved salvation, her soul magnified the Lord and her spirit exulted in God's saving act." What is meant by the spirit? It designates, in different places of the Bible, "the substance of the soul," or its "superior part," or even the faculty of imagination. Here it stands for "the soul in what is highest in it." In sum, "because her spirit exulted interiorly, her soul magnified [the Lord] aloud; and thus it expressed exultation for the past and magnification for the present, exultation being naturally first."

The motive for Mary's song of praise is twofold. It comes from "the benefit of grace which made her lovable to God and praiseworthy to men." All will praise her as blessed for the grace she received, as more blessed for her intent to keep her virginity, and as "most blessed for the privilege of her fecundity." Mary's motive for praise also comes from the miracle of the divine power, which was "great and pious." As great, it did great things in her, for the "mystery of the Incarnation is great and inscrutable." As pious, it "did holy and pious things to show the holiness of his Name." And thus was the Virgin magnified and sanctified in the conception" of her Son.

The mode and scope of Mary's praise of the Lord refer to the extent of this praise:

> It consists in praising the divine mercy as regards human redemption, which is already inchoate in the conception by the Virgin. The work of our redemption proclaims mercy and power, and it manifests generosity and truth: mercy in revealing the human fall, power in vanquishing the devil, generosity in sharing the Holy Spirit, and truth in fulfilling the promise.

These four points are then looked at in turn. Mercy (*et misericordia ejus . . .*) which is "liberating and saving, extends only to those who fear," this being of course the fear of God, a virtue recommended in the Old Testament. The power resides in the Lord's arm (*in brachio suo*), which in fact is the Son. By it the proud are scattered. These are the demons, who, unlike humans, are vanquished once and for all. "True generosity" (*esurientes implevit bonis et divites dimisit inanes*) consists in giving "to the poor, not to the wealthy." Finally, Mary anticipates the fulfilment of the promise (*suscepit Israel puerum suum*): in Israel "there was sent ahead of time the fulfilment of the promise, which was made by the divine benignity and fulfilled by the divine truth." The Lord could never forget this (*recordatus misericordiae suae*). The true promise had been made to the patriarchs and to Abraham. For, as Bonaventure points out, this verse should be construed: "As he spoke to the patriarchs, and as he spoke especially to Abraham and to his seed, in which the age of nature and the age of the written law are touched." Yet another construction is possible: "He received Israel, mindful of his mercy to Abraham and to his seed, as he spoke to the patriarchs." In any case, Abraham is named personally because the promise was made to him at first. And "the faithful are the seed of Abraham."

Bonaventure sums up the sense of Mary's song in these words:

> Hence the blessed Virgin begins her song with the greatness of the highest principle and ends it with the eternity of the end; for she praises the one who is alpha and omega, the principle and the end; and this is indeed right, since in this song she shows the consummation of all the promised benefits, and thus her song is the consummation of all praises and songs and even of the Scriptures.

The Genealogy

The genealogy of Jesus is in fact not the occasion for extensive Marian considerations. Bonaventure remarks that, after the sacramental episode of Jesus's baptism by John, which illustrates the eternal origin of the divine Word, Luke proceeds to assert the reality of the Incarnation, for the "temporal genealogy" of Christ renders totally impossible the purely spiritualistic views of the humanity taken from the Virgin Mary that were fashionable in the docetic heresy. Like all readers, however, Bonaventure faces the problem that the genealogy, by omitting all mention of Mary, sounds as though Joseph were the true natural father of Jesus. On the contrary,

Luke's genealogy shows that "according to his temporal generation, [Jesus] had no true, but only a putative, father, since he was born of the Virgin."[6] The genealogy in fact tallies with Luke's central concern in his Gospel: he intends to focus attention on

> the priesthood of Christ, by which we are reconciled from the state of sin into adoption as children, which is indeed done through sacramental regeneration; and therefore he follows up Christ's adoptive or legal filiation, ascending up to God, and this through seventy-seven degrees, since by this number, as Augustine says, the universality of sins is designated. . . . For this reason he placed the genealogy, not at the start of his book, but after the baptism of Christ.

By contrast, Matthew focusses attention on "the reign and the humanity of Christ, in which he succeeded David; and therefore one deals with his descent down to the reception of our flesh." Matthew's forty generations designate the universality of time. And "since the begetting of Christ according to the flesh is the beginning of the Gospel, it is placed at the start of the book."

Whatever the differences between the two genealogies —Bonaventure lists seven of them—the absence of Mary suggests that "the genealogy contributes nothing to the truth of Christ." This, however, is not so. One could respond with the Venerable Bede, who himself follows St Jerome, that "it is not the custom of the Scriptures to include women in genealogies." One could also maintain that, Joseph and Mary being of the same tribe, the genealogy of the one applies also to the other. If the first point is correct, then "it appears from it that little is mentioned in Scripture about Mary. For if there is no mention of her in the genealogy, in keeping with the customs of the Scriptures, where it would seem to be all but necessary, still less should there be anything concerning her own actions."

Bonaventure then attempts to explain this reticence of the Scriptures to speak of Mary in particular by its general reluctance to speak of women. In so doing, he embarks on what must undoubtedly be the most anti-feminist passage of his entire writings. He argues from the multiple "defects" of women, some of which are natural and real according to the science and philosophy of Aristotle, which still generally prevailed in the thirteenth century, others being symbolic and imaginary, others still, institutional or historical:

> There is no mention of women in the genealogies because of a defect in nature, since "woman is a missed out male" [Aristotle]; and because of a defect in meaning, since woman does not signify Christ, but the *Ecclesia*, not the higher part of reason, but the lower (1 Cor 11:3); and because of a defect in function, since it does not belong to her to teach or preside; and because of a defect in healing, since it does not belong to her to heal, but to be healed; and because of a defect in principle, since "it is not the male who is from woman, but woman from the male" (1 Cor 11:8); and because of the memory of the first sin: "not Adam was seduced, but woman."

There would in fact be no difficulty to show that

Bonaventure takes a more favorable view of woman in other sections of his works.[7] The point here is that he has to deal with what must have been, in the eyes of the pious faithful of his time, an astonishing fact: the discrepancy between the high place of Mary in Christian devotion and her subdued image in the Gospels. This, as Bonaventure understands it, is not due to anything that affects Mary directly and personally; it derives from the broader problem of the actual situation of woman in society and theology. Furthermore, Bonaventure attempts to balance the picture, at least in regard to Mary, by pointing out that there are women in the Old Testament from whose story one can learn about Mary. In other words, there exists a legitimate Marian typology, through which Mary is more present in the Scriptures than meets the eye at first sight:

> And for that reason the [genealogical] descent does not go through women; hence it is not the custom in the Scriptures to make much mention of Mary; and because the Gospels began with the forerunner... and also for the said reasons. Something was nonetheless written in the Old Testament which could be an image of the Virgin in several women, who bore the image of Mary and of the *Ecclesia*.

Mary as Contemplative

Not only in the Old Testament does Bonaventure meet with types of the Virgin Mary. Some women of the New Testament also present a vantage point from which the Mother of God is seen in better light. The episode of Luke 10:38-42, in which Jesus pays a visit to Martha and

Mary, becomes the occasion, not only for a dissertation on the relative merits of the active and the contemplative lives, respectively represented by Martha and by Mary, but also for extolling the Virgin Mary as the model of both the active and the contemplative lives.

"As Christ was corporally present as a guest, he is spiritually present to the active and the contemplative."[8] Bonaventure develops the familiar comparison and contrast between Martha and Mary. The former is "a good active person, shunning leisure," the other being "perfect in the leisure of contemplation." Mary sits humbly at the feet of Jesus; she experiences abundant fruits of devotion, for "the work of a contemplative soul is to cultivate the tears of compunction and devotion." The contest between the two is brought about by "laborious" Martha's complaint against "leisurely" Mary. Yet the latter neither responds nor even takes side. "It pertains to the contemplative not to argue but rather to be silent, to listen, and to meditate." But "Mary lost nothing by her silence, since the Lord took her side by defending her." The solution of the conflict is that "the contemplative life should be elected without regrets. Martha, however—that is, the active life—should be pursued by necessity." Martha's imperfection is marked by three defects: "worry in thought, trouble in feeling, division in action." As Bonaventure remarks, "all these impede us from totally tending toward God." By contrast, only one thing is necessary: "the kingdom of God; and when one has it, nothing is lacking":

> Therefore, the contemplative life is simply more to be desired, as being better and to be elected for

oneself, and as being safer, sweeter, and more stable; the active life, however, is not to be despised, but according to place and time it is to be elected from time to time, as being prior, more painful, and more fecund; it is useful for oneself and for others. . . . Therefore the spirituals should sometimes go out, sometimes go in, sometimes go up, sometimes go down, as was seen by Jacob (Gen 28).

At this point of his reflections, Bonaventure introduces the image of the Virgin Mary. He does so for a liturgical reason which does remain extraneous to the text of Scripture as such, though it relates to the resonance of this text in the Church's life of prayer. As Bonaventure notes, "the custom is to read this Gospel for the Assumption of the Virgin." This custom in fact prevailed in the Catholic Church until June 26, 1951, when the Congregation of Rites introduced a different text for the Mass, where the traditional Gospel was replaced by Luke 1:41-50: the Visitation and the *Magnificat*.

The relevance of Lk 10:38-42 to Mary's Assumption is even more to be noted as our investigation of Bonaventure's Mariology has not yet found any discussion by the Seraphic Doctor of this feast and of the corresponding doctrine. Bonaventure looks for the reasons of this liturgical choice. The end of the Gospel—about choosing the better part—"was said literally of Mary Magdalen, but applies more truly to the Virgin Mary." Or also, "in these two sisters the perfection of the active and the contemplative lives was described, which was most perfectly realized in the Virgin. For what was given to these two sisters separately was given to Mary totally and integrally." Or again, this text explains two ways of receiving Christ, corporally and spiritually, in an external house and in one's interior house. "And this double reception was most perfect in Mary, who received him in the nuptial bed of her body, fed him, nurtured him, educated him, and assiduously served him; and she also received him in the nuptial bed of her heart, as she saw, believed, loved and imitated him."

Finally, Luke's Gospel shows up "three things which were most perfect in the Virgin Mary: hospitality in the village, service in Martha, cohabitation in Mary." The Virgin Mary is the model of the three. She is like a "village protected by the towers of the virtues." She also, "though she was the Mother, made herself handmaiden and servant." And, in conclusion:

> Mary was right in cohabiting or contemplating. For, like the other Mary, she stood near to Christ [at the cross]. . . . She was the Virgin who came the nearest to him, who therefore received his words best and preserved them for others. . . . Hence she was rightly designated by the Ark of the Covenant . . . for the devotion of her charity, and by the stick of Aaron for the rectitude of her virtue, and by the Table of the Testimony for her great knowledge of the contemplation of the truth. And she was contemplative above all.

Bonaventure's conclusion may seem to go somewhat beyond his premises: "This Gospel was appropriated to the Assumption of the Virgin, not by human invention but by divine inspiration." Yet it at least illustrates the seriousness of his reflection on Mary's Assumption as the climax of God's gifts to her and as the appropriate crowning point of her life and holiness:

> Mary chose the better part both in grace and in glory, in which the perfect and proper praise of the Virgin comes to a close. . . . Therefore she alone is the best among women with absolute superabundance. . . .

Notes

1. The Commentary on Luke is in vol. VII of the Quaracchi edition; the other biblical commentaries are in vol. VI. There are very few studies of Bonaventure as an exegete. One may consult Thomas Reist, *Saint Bonaventure as a Biblical Commentator. A Translation and Analysis of his Commentary on Luke, XVIII, 34 - XIX, 42,* (Washington: University Press of America, 1985).

2. *In Lucam,* prologue, (vol. II, p. 3-11). Rather than document each reference separately, I will group a number of them under one footnote, as already remarked, ch. 2, note 2.

3. l. c., ch. 1, n. 44-45 (p. 21-22).

4. On the Annunciation: l. c., ch. 1, n. 40-68 (p. 20-26).

5. On the Visitation: l. c., ch. 1, n. 71-93 (p. 27-32).

6. On the Genealogy: l. c., ch. 3, n. 57-63 (p. 85-88).

7. See the reference above, ch. 2, note 9.

8. On Martha and Mary: l. c., ch. 10, n. 38-80 (p. 273-277).

CHAPTER 5

MARY IN
ST JOHN'S GOSPEL

Bonaventure's commentary on the *Gospel of John* is of another character than his commentary on *Luke*. It is much shorter. Yet it also presents an aspect that would be more readily associated with the task of a "bachelor of the Sentences" than with that of a mere biblical bachelor. For, unlike the commentary on *Luke*, which proceeds entirely by analysis and explanation of the text, the commentary on *John*, after a brief analysis and explanation of a passage, often continues in question form in the scholastic mode. The questions are succinctly put, and the answers are equally condensed. Yet the tone is more in tune with the scholastic method of theological argumentation than with the expository way of explanation. One may therefore think that the commentary on *Luke*, elaborate though it is, remains nearer to what Bonaventure must have done in his instructions on the Bible when he was only a biblical bachelor (which he became most probably in 1248); whereas the commentary on *John*, in

spite of its brevity, is nearer to what Bonaventure must
have taught about the Bible as a bachelor of the Sentences
(from 1250 on) and as master-regent at the Franciscan
theologate of Paris (1254-1257). The final difference
between the two commentaries derives from the author's
having adopted two different methods when he finalized
his texts, some time after the actual teaching of them.
In doing the Gospel of Luke he was more concerned
about general readers and preachers than about students.
In doing the Gospel of John he was chiefly thinking of
theological students: for preachers he composed his
second Johannine volume, the *Sermons (collationes) on the
Gospel of John:* these are outlines for sermons on selected
themes of the Gospel. Even with these differences, however, the treatment of the biblical text remains quite
similar to what we have found in relation to *Luke:* quotations of and allusions to all sorts of passages from the Old
and the New Testaments, which Bonaventure relates
somehow to the point under survey, and numerous
references to previous Fathers, theologians, and com-
mentators.

Our own look at Bonaventure's reflections on *John* will
have to be, like these reflections themselves, brief. We
will examine the two works together, most of the Marian
material being in the *commentary* rather than in the
collationes.

The Wedding at Cana

This is the only Marian passage in the Gospel of John
which Bonaventure selects for special attention. According to an opinion which he accepts on the authority of

St Jerome and St Augustine, the wedding at Cana was that of John, the apostle and evangelist. Mary is not said to have been invited. But John was related to her, and so "she went, for reasons of kinship, in order to oblige, just as she went to the mountain to Elizabeth in order to help her."[1] For the same reason of kinship, Jesus was invited. What the exact kinship was, Bonaventure does not explain; but in the Middle Ages it was widely held that Mary was John's maternal aunt. Later, speaking of the women who were present at the Crucifixion, Bonaventure writes: "It is to be noted that Ann is said to have had three husbands, Joachim, Cleophas, and Salome; and from these three husbands she had three Mary's: the Mother of the Lord, who was Joachim's daughter; the mother of James, who was Cleophas's daughter; and the mother of Simon and Jude, who was Salome's daughter." In this case, there were several relatives of Jesus in the group of the apostles; and this may explain why, at John's wedding, "the Lord was present with his disciples." That John was also widely believed to have remained a virgin is not an insuperable objection. For then John would have been in the same position as Mary in relation to her marriage: "Like the Virgin Mary, he entrusted himself to the will of the Holy Spirit, so that the virgin who was to serve the Virgin [i.e., after the Crucifixion, when he received Mary into his house], would be similar to the Virgin in the way of virginity."

Be that as it may, Mary noticed that they were running short of wine, and, "having pity on the bridegroom's poverty," asked for a miracle. It was as though she had told Christ, "Fill up their want with your abundance; for she knew that he was rich in mercy and power, although

he seemed to be destitute." Bonaventure is aware of a
subtle dialectic at work here. For, "the Lord, hinting to
his Mother that neither could she, as his Mother, order
him to do so, nor could he, as her son, do so except at the
proper time," said to her: "What is it to me and to you,
woman?"

This expression retains the commentator's attention.
Why does Christ call Mary, "woman," rather than,
"mother"? The answer is unexpected, in that, rather than
seeing the word as a rebuke, Bonaventure reads it as
justifying her request:

> He calls her woman, not on account of any weakness,
> but in reference to her nature and sex. For this is
> the woman of whom it is said in *Proverbs*: "Who will
> find a strong woman"?[2] As though he said: "You
> have power to ask for this as a holy woman, not as
> a mother."

In any case, "it is not yet opportune to do it." The hour
that has not yet come is that of Jesus's "illumination
and passion."

Mary, however, is sufficiently attuned to her Son's
unexpressed thoughts to understand that this is not a
refusal: "She knew that he could; she also knew that he
knew; she knew that he would, because he always obeyed
her." Accordingly, Mary gave the proper directives to
the servants: "His Mother, knowing that this response
was not given from indignation, but from humility and
for instruction, confidently gave orders."

Further explanation is given, in a special "question,"
regarding the import of "What is it to me and to you"?

This answer was "not insulting but instructive." The Mother of the Lord intervened in favor of their poor relatives, asking for a miracle. The answer mixed reproof with approval:

> The Lord showed in his response that she must not ask for this as a mother, since he could not do it by the power of the nature he had taken from her; therefore he says to her, *woman*, not *mother*. She must not ask in favor of relatives, like one who cares for kinship of the flesh; therefore he says: *What is it to me and to you?* He shows that a miracle should not be done to remedy want, but to manifest his glory, the necessity of which was not yet there; therefore he says: *My hour has not yet come.* Since, however, the woman who asked was holy, and since those for whom she asked were poor, and since his glory had to be manifested to his disciples, therefore he listened to her.

So far, Bonaventure has focussed attention chiefly on what he identified as the literal sense of the biblical passage. This is proper in a rapid commentary which, even if it raises certain critical questions, does not attempt to examine them at length. But medieval reflection is seldom confined to the literal sense. Medieval preaching never is. For the listeners' edification it liked to investigate also the moral sense: what does the text imply in regard to Christian behavior? It also delved into the allegorical or analogical sense: what does the text imply, in the analogy of faith, regarding the doctrines that relate to Christ and salvation? The wedding was celebrated at Cana "on the third day." Already in his commentary on this verse (*John* 2:1), Bonaventure wonders at the implications of this third day. Allegorically, "there are three kinds of days, according to the three kinds of time: in nature, in the Law, and in grace." At the time of grace, the third day is when "a wedding took place between Christ and the Church at the assumption of the flesh [by the divine Word]." In this marriage, "six vases with insipid and nutritionless water were changed into tasty and joyful wine": the shadow of the Law into the truth, the multitude of sacrifices into unity, the hardness of sorrows into gladness, enigmas into clarity, terrors into love, promises into acquisition. "And all this was done in answer to the Virgin's prayers as she interceded." In the moral sense, the wedding is that of "God and the soul in her reconciliation with God." Jesus was invited; the wine of "internal devotion" ran out, as when "man becomes dry and without devotion"; but "at the prayers of the Virgin, who has compassion on those who are miserable, God fills the vases with the water of compunction, which is changed into the suavity of devotion." Furthermore, the vases in question are no other than "consideration," or meditation, as it considers our lack of knowledge, our lack of wariness, our lack of "internal consolation," our lack of resistance, our lack of certainty in expectation. "Then these vases are filled to the brim with water, when the penitent soul washes her bed night after night with these considerations. And from water the excellent wine of devotion is made."

In his *Homily n. 8* on the Gospel of John, Bonaventure reflects again on the spiritual symbolism of the wedding at Cana. Although marriage between a man and a woman was instituted by God in paradise and was consecrated by the presence of Christ at Cana as the scene of his first miracle, yet the main lesson of this passage is to be found at another level. For "there is a marriage of God and the soul, and this entails a wedding of grace. And there is a marriage of Jesus Christ and the Church, and this entails today the wedding of the Eucharist as a banquet, and in the future the wedding of glory like a supper."[3] These three spiritual weddings take place "in the nuptial bed of conscience, in the tabernacle of the Church, in the palace of glory." The wedding at Cana of Galilee corresponds particularly well to the "spiritual nuptials of God and the soul." For Cana means "zeal," and Galilee means "transmigration, that is, transient, or wheel, that is, quick." This enables Bonaventure to suggest this spiritual interpretation of the episode:

> These nuptials take place in the conscience of the soul that has the zeal of love, which soul migrates to the mountain of the Lord with the devotion of her mind, and is quick with the swiftness of her action. In these nuptials the Lord changes the water of tears into the wine of consolation, especially if the Mother of Jesus is there.

Such a wedding is, as Bonaventure adds, that of religious in their matrimonial commitment to the Lord.

Bonaventure opens *Homily n. 9* with the exclamation: "O how good it is to invite to one's banquet the Mother of Jesus, who brings to the banquet's poor the solace of compassion, the counsel of instruction, the suffrage of prayer!"[4] Mary says: "They have no wine." When we hear this we can think of the wine of nature, which is to be used moderately, or of the "abominable wine of guilt," which is followed by the triple wine of remorse, of eternal damnation, and of temporal calamities and miseries. But we can also think of the "fourfold wine of grace." Not without humor, Bonaventure now lists four different wines that were presumably fashionable in Paris in the middle of the thirteenth century. He calls them "raspé," "rosé," "salmet," and "claret": the "raspé of compunction, . . . the rosé of compassion, . . . the salmet of devotion, . . . the claret or scented juice of internal fruition." This "wine of grace should be desired," for it is "healthy, . . . strengthening, . . . and joyful." It was paid for at the inn by the good Samaritan. . . .

* * * * *

No other major text of the *Gospel of John* draws Bonaventure's attention to the Virgin Mary. There are only occasional allusions to her in other parts of the Commentary and the Homilies. I will mention only a few, which will complete the picture of Mary insofar as the works of the Seraphic Doctor have extracted it from the New Testament.

At the Passion of Jesus, those who felt no compassion, even among the disciples, stayed far away, while those who loved him the more remained the nearer to him. These were "his Mother, who felt compassion more than all, . . . his Mother's sister, Mary of Cleophas, . . . and Mary Magdalen, named after the town of Magdala. These three women, being the most compassionate, stood next to the cross of the Lord."[5] Yet John was not far away, since Jesus saw him and commended him to his Mother as he commended her to him. John received her *in suam* ("in her . . .").

One could conceivably complete the sentence with the word "house," to the effect that John received Mary in his house. Bonaventure remarks that Augustine reads, in his Bible (which in fact coincides both with the Latin Vulgate and with the Greek text): *in sua*, that is, in "what was his." Yet, using a different Latin construction, he himself prefers to complete the sentence with the word, *matrem* (mother): "He received her as his, that is, as his Mother, in order to honor, protect, and serve her as a son his Mother."

In *Homily n. 10*, commenting on the Temple which Jesus will rebuild in three days, Bonaventure lists several spiritual meanings of the temple: there are the temple of glory, the temple of the Church, the temple of the faithful soul, the temple of the virginal womb, and the temple of the humanity of Christ. The temple of the virginal womb was prophesied about in Ezechiel 43:4: "The majesty of God entered the temple by way of the gate which is facing the east." In his commentary, Bonaventure identifies

the majesty of God with the fulness of the Divinity, the temple with the virginal womb, the east with the heavenly court, the gate with constant devotion, the way which brings God with true humility, since "He looked at the humility of his handmaiden."[6]

Of the temple of the virginal womb it may be further said that it was "dedicated to God in sanctification, . . . adorned in conversion, . . . and dwelt in at the Incarnation." In particular, it was adorned with good thoughts, these being the "side windows" of 3 *Kings* 6:4,[7] "through which the light entered": they are "the holy meditations through which the divine illuminations entered the soul." The temple of the virginal womb was also adorned with holy affections: the gold of charity, for the "Virgin's affections were all informed by charity." It was finally adorned with virtuous works. . . .

It is not enough for Bonaventure, at this point, to identify the Virgin as a spiritual temple of the Lord. His *Homily n. 53* goes much farther. Here Bonaventure reflects on the words of Jesus: "I will pray the Father, and he will send you another Paraclete." This Paraclete is the Holy Spirit, as Bonaventure, following the text of John 14:16, duly recognizes. Yet he looks further at the meaning of the word, paraclete, or "advocate."[8] And he remarks that "the Lord has given us a triple advocate in our favor," with the threefold tasks, respectively, of "fighting, speaking for us, and interceding":

> The first advocate is Christ. . . . The second advocate is the Holy Spirit. . . . The third advocate is the most blessed Virgin. She is the advocate of intercession, who, in order better to move the judge, shows her female sex. She is the Esther at whose sight the king's heart was changed into kindness, as is prefigured in *Esther* 15:11. She is the one to whom the Church sings, *Eia ergo, advocata nostra* [Oh, our Advocate].

That Mary acts as our advocate of intercession, along with the Savior and the Holy Spirit, our first paracletes or advocates, is not, however, as extravagant as it sounds. For Bonaventure qualifies it immediately in regard to the nature of their advocacy:

Having therefore the Son as our advocate who fights, the Spirit as our advocate who speaks for us, the Queen of virgins as our advocate who intercedes, let us safely entrust our cause to them in regard to *law*, if at least we have corrected the *fact*, for, in what touches fact, an advocate does not redeem his clients' error.

In other words, the advocacy of the Virgin, as that of Christ and of the Holy Spirit, does not exempt the faithful from what the theological language of the Scholastics called "doing what is in them." It was presumably neither the place nor the time, in such a sermon, to discuss the intricacies of the doctrine of grace. All good action is by grace; it is even by Christ. For "spiritual motion and feeling flow from Christ the head into us in some spiritual way." The "fulness of sufficiency" is found in every one who is just, the "fulness of abundance" in every perfect man, the "fulness of excellence" in the most blessed Virgin; but this is only because "the fulness of super-flowing is found in Christ, from whom . . . we all have received."

Undoubtedly, Bonaventure's exegesis of the Marian texts of the New Testament differs considerably from the use of holy Scripture in the theology and even the Mariology of the twentieth century. A comparison of his findings with such a volume as *Mary in the New Testament*,[9] a modern cooperative study made by an ecumenical team of scholars, would be, from this point of view, instructive, though it would hardly help our appreciation of the Bonaventurian approach. This approach to the picture of Mary in the New Testament is marked by four prominent features.

Firstly, Bonaventure makes considerable use of a typological reading of the Old Testament. Many texts, whatever their significance in their immediate and original context, also refer to the story of Jesus as told in the New Testament. And the typology in question is discovered backward, by looking for illustrative material in the books of the old Hebrew tradition, rather than forward, by looking for material of the early Christian tradition that would show the fulfilment of prophecies or promises made or implied under the Old Covenant.

Secondly, the typology of which Bonaventure, along with scholastic theology in general, is so fond, can be of the three kinds which medieval exegesis distinguished: analogical (also called allegorical), tropological (or moral), and anagogical. The first two spiritual senses have appeared the most frequently. Yet the anagogical dimension of Scripture is never far from Bonaventure's concerns, since it refers to the dimension of eschatology as this can already be experienced in this life by participation and anticipation. Analogy is, as it were, the flower of faith; tropology is that of love; anagogy that of hope. The three theological virtues are constantly at work in this exegesis. It is therefore not surprising that they should discover in Scripture what a sober objective look at the literal meaning of the biblical texts would not unearth.

Thirdly, the Bonaventurian conception of the literal sense of Scripture is quite at variance with the literal reading done in our own days with the tools of scientific exegesis. Bonaventure tends to take the letter of the text at face-value when it is read uncritically. Indeed, he is aware of variant opinions as to the exact sense of various texts or as to the historical context or the geographical location of some of the biblical events. He takes side or not, depending in part on the relative importance of the problem and its relevance to the piety of faith, in part on the secondary evidence that can be marshalled out of such traditional lights of biblical scholarship as St Jerome and, more recently, the often anonymous authors of the *glossa* (a more or less literal paraphrase and interpretation of Scripture) and Peter Comestor (d. c. 1179), whose *Historia scholastica* was treated as a source-book of information for biblical history.

Finally, at a different level, the liturgical practice of the Church had to be taken into account. Bonaventure assumed that this practice had itself been, if not formally inspired, at least providentially guided, by the Holy Spirit. For further light on the relevance of liturgy in Bonaventure's Mariology, we should now turn to his views of the cult of Mary and to the homilies that he preached on the major feasts of the Virgin.

Notes

1. On the wedding at Cana: *Commentary in Johannem*, ch. 2, n. 1-17 (vol. VI, p. 267-283).

2. This point will be explored at length in the *Lectures on the Gifts of the Holy Spirit;* see below, ch. 10.

3. *Collationes in Johannem*, 8 (p. 545-547).

4. l. c., 9 (p. 547).

5. *Comm. in Johannem*, ch. 19, n. 37-39 (p. 497-498). For further considerations on this word of Jesus on the cross, see below, ch. 10.

6. *Collationes*, 10 (p. 548-549).

7. This is 1*Kings* 6:4 in most modern translations, 3 *Kings* being the nomenclature of the Latin Vulgate.

8. *Collationes,* 53 (p. 602-603).

9. Raymond Brown et al., *Mary in the New Testament,* (New York: Paulist, 1978).

Part Three

Liturgical Piety

CHAPTER 6

THE CULT OF MARY

There are two basic ways to look at Bonaventure's Marian piety as it relates to liturgical practice. One way is to read and analyze the sermons preached by the Seraphic Doctor for the feasts of the Virgin Mary. A number of these have been preserved. They refer to the four basic liturgical feasts of Mary that were generally observed in the thirteenth century, namely—in their liturgical sequence— the feasts of Mary's Purification (February 2), of the Annunciation (March 25), of her Assumption into heaven (August 15), and of her Nativity (September 8). Bonaventure preached on the occasion of these feasts on what must have been a regular basis, and the relevant homilies will be studied in our next chapter.

The other way toward assessing Bonaventure's Marian liturgical piety is to listen to his important remarks on the principles that should regulate the cult of Mary. This matter occupies his attention in book III of the Commentary on the Sentences, as a side-issue of Christology.

The question was introduced by the previous question of the cult of Christ. Distinction VIII had focused on a comparison of the two nativities of Christ, in eternity and in time. This naturally led to the question whether the adoration of Christ is addressed to his human or to his divine nature. And this in turn led to a broader consideration of *latria* as prayer of adoration. Bonaventure carefully, if briefly, examined the cult of the icons or images of Christ, of the Mother of Christ, of the cross, of the saints in general and, along with the saints, of the angels. This investigation provides the topic of the present chapter.

Bonaventure's broad approach to the question is clearly dependent on a problematic that had dominated Christian life and thought in the Western Church since the time of Emperor Charlemagne. This problematic may be briefly illustrated with the help of the "Caroline books," even though these books are never directly quoted by Bonaventure. The Caroline books, issued around the time of the Council of Frankfort of 794, had been composed by several theologians of the court of Charlemagne, as a critique of the cult of icons endorsed by the seventh ecumenical council (II Council of Nicaea, of 786). Generally speaking, the Frankish theologians followed the principles previously formulated by Pope Gregory the Great in a letter to the bishop of Marseille: pictures are useful for the instruction of the simple, both to give them the knowledge of what they cannot read and to nurture piety and devotion; but they should have no place in worship as such. Bonaventure's position, however, is not entirely identical with that of Gregory the Great and of the Caroline books.

* * * * *

The question of adoration is raised by Bonaventure in the context of the Christological concept called "the communication of idioms." This expression relates to the relationships between the divine and the human natures as they are united in the Person of the Word made flesh. The "idioms" (in Greek) are the qualities properly pertaining to each nature. The "communication" is the sharing of these qualities, or of some of them, between the two natures. The concept of the communication of idioms tries to elucidate the language of Scripture and of the theological and devotional tradition: Is it legitimate to speak of the human nature of Jesus as though it shared the divine attributes? Reversely, is it right to speak of the divine nature of the Word of God as though it shared the creaturely limitations of the human nature? These difficult questions had retained the attention of theologians since the time of the Christological controversies in the fourth century. They were broached during the discussions between Nestorius and his orthodox opponents, before and after the Council of Ephesus (431).

Without entering unnecessary details, it will be enough to mention that Bonaventure understands the proper communication of idioms—the proper language to be used in regard to the two natures of Christ and their shared qualities—as being "not convergence (*convenientia*) in nature, but convergence in the Person."[1] In other words, the two natures in Christ are not related to each other directly; rather, each is immediately related to the divine Person of the Word: thus, it is the divine Person, not the divine nature, that is incarnate of the Virgin Mary. After looking at *latria* in relation to the humanity of Christ,

Bonaventure will therefore look at it in relation to the Mother of Jesus as the Forthbringer of God (*Dei Genitrix*). The entire d. 9 deals with these matters of worship, on the following pattern:

d. 9, a. 1: "Adoration as related to the one who is adored."

q. 1: "Whether a cult of *latria* must be practiced before the humanity or the flesh of Christ."

q. 2: "Whether a cult of *latria* must be practiced before the image of Christ."

q. 3: "Whether a cult of *latria* must be practiced before the Mother of Christ."

q. 4: "Whether a cult of *latria* must be practiced before the cross of Christ."

q. 5: "Whether a cult of *latria* must be practiced before the members of Christ."

q. 6: "Whether a cult of *latria* may be practiced without sin before Christ's adversary."

a. 2: "*Latria* itself in what it is." Bonaventure asks if *latria* is a virtue (q. 1), a general or special virtue (q. 2), a cardinal or theological virtue (q. 3), and whether it is distinct from *dulia* (q. 4).

Latria generally designates the attitude of worship that is due only to God. *Dulia* corresponds to the honor that should be appropriately rendered to the saints. Moreover, in Bonaventure's vocabulary at this point, the word "adoration" is used in a broad sense: it can cover *dulia* as well as *latria*; but it is distinguished from veneration or honor, in that it is a special form of *oratio*, or prayer, which, as he explains, veneration is not.[2]

The adoration of Christ will not detain us. It is enough to note on what principle such adoration is justified: the communication of idioms. In and by itself, the humanity of Jesus deserves no more than *dulia*; it should be offered *latria* insofar as it is united to the Person of the Word: "Because there is one Person in Christ, to which supreme reverence is due, it should be adored with one adoration, *latria*, in regard to both natures, the divinity and the humanity."[3]

In the following, q. 2, Bonaventure extends to the pictures of Christ the same adoration of *latria*. While he makes no mention of the iconoclastic controversy, of Pope Gregory's letter to the bishop of Marseille, or of the Caroline books, he draws on the *De fide orthodoxa* of St John of Damascus; and his remarks can easily be related to the traditional problem of the worship of icons. Pictures, Bonaventure believes, were introduced into the church "for a reasonable cause," which he identifies with the need to instruct the simple, to remedy the slowness of affective devotion, which is better excited by sight than by hearing, and to help the weakness of memory, which remembers better what is seen than what is heard. "Therefore, by divine dispensation, it happened that pictures were made, especially in churches, so that seeing them, we should remember the benefits extended to us and the virtuous works of the saints." Yet Bonaventure reaches much further. Going far beyond Gregory's letter and the Caroline books, he extends the cult of *latria* to the images of Christ. For the image is meant to "represent the one who was crucified for us"; it is not given to us "for itself, but for him." Therefore, "all the reverence which is exhibited to it is shown to Christ," who himself deserves *latria*. This is supported by Augustine in *De doctrina christiana*, ch. 9.

Bonaventure repeats this point in his answers to objections. "When the image is adored, it is not adored by virtue of the nobility it has in itself, but by virtue of the nobility it signifies in itself" (ad 3). An image differs from a human person in that "the honor offered a person is not entirely referred to the archetype, as is the case with the honor offered a painted or sculpted image" (ad 4).

Admittedly, images can be an occasion of abuse and of idolatry. But so can Scripture:

> Although the sacred Letters have been and are to this date, at times, an occasion of error, they should not for that reason be erased and creatures destroyed, because it pertains to the divine judgment that they be for the good of those who are good and also for the evil of those who are evil. And so should one think concerning images (ad 5).

This clearly implies a close parallelism between holy Scripture and the holy icons, including—a Western emphasis which is at variance with the Eastern one—sculptures and statues.

Finally, facing the objection that this view of pictures is not founded in Scripture, Bonaventure states that, in keeping with 1 Cor 2:2 and 2 Thes 2:14, "the apostles handed on many things that were not written." Then, on the authority of John of Damascus, he argues that the cult of images derives from "divine traditions and apostolic sanctions," not from "inventions." This is based explicitly on the Abgar legend (Jesus sent his picture to king Abgar) and on the Luke legend (Luke painted pictures of both Jesus and Mary): John of Damascus is cited in support of this information (ad 6).

This brings us to the cult of Mary, the subject matter of q. 3. Is the Mother of Christ entitled, like the icons of Christ, to *latria*?

Bonaventure grounds his response in two principles. The first is factual: "The most blessed Virgin Mary is a mere creature; therefore she does not ascend to a cult of *latria*." The second is Christological: though a creature, she is the Mother of God (*Dei mater*). She has "a most excellent name, than which a more excellent one cannot belong to a mere creature." This justifies, in her case, *hyperdulia*. Bonaventure explains this name: "The living Virgin is *Dei mater*." It is due to this that "not only those on the way (*viatores*) but also the blessed ones (*comprehensores*), not only humans but also angels, revere her with a special prerogative. For, by being the Mother of God, she has been made superior to the other creatures; and it is proper to honor and venerate her above the others." The special cult of Mary, *hyperdulia*, is entirely founded on the traditional title given to her for Christological reasons, as confirmed by the Council of Ephesus (which, however, is not mentioned at this point).

Answering some objections, Bonaventure does not consider the minimalist position that would exclude Mary from any kind of cult. No such opinion is recorded, and one may presume that it was not a live theological or liturgical option at the time. The only position that is cited for refutation is one that would identify the cult of Mary with that of the pictures of Christ. *Latria* offered to the icon goes in reality to "the prototype." Why can it not be the same with the Virgin? (arg. 1). A Christotypical view of Mary would seem to favor this argument. In his reply, ad 1, Bonaventure distinguishes between two sorts of references to a first: the honor given can be referred to another as to its proper subject or as to its final end. The first case is that of the icons of Christ: "The honor by which we adore the image of Christ is referred to him as to its subject." The second case is that of the Virgin. "Hence, one who adores the image of Christ adores Christ, not the image; but one who adores the Mother of Christ adores both Christ and his Mother." One and the same veneration of the Virgin includes adoration of Christ by *latria* as its main and final purpose and adoration of Mary by *dulia*. Thus the cult of Mary is not a simple affair. Because of the analogous meaning of adoration and the twofold attitude that is intrinsic to its practice, it may easily turn into a source of confusion.

Another argument in favor of a Marian cult of *latria* starts from the belief that, when Mary was made the Mother of God, she also became "the Mother of all creatures." The Son of God gave her dominion over the universe; and *latria* is commensurate to the majesty of this dominion (arg. 2). Bonaventure, however, does not at this point endorse Mary's universal motherhood.[4] Mary received from Christ "a dominion of presidency," not one "of majesty and omnipotence." The latter belongs to the Son alone and is not communicable to a mere creature (ad 2). Therefore the cult of Mary must not be *latria*.

Still, one can consider that "the flesh of Christ is consubstantial with that of the Virgin." As *latria* is due to the first, it should also be offered the second (arg. 3). Yet this is a fallacy, a "paralogism on an accident" (*paralogismus accidentiae*) which confuses two aspects of the "flesh of the Word": it is "not as human flesh, but as flesh assumed" (by the divine Word) that this flesh is adored with *latria*. But there is no such assumption of Mary's flesh by the Word (ad. 3).

Again, it is indeed true that since Christ honored his Mother, we should do the same (arg. 4). Yet "Christ did not adore her with *latria* but with *hyperdulia*, not as a goddess but as his Mother." It follows that "Christ teaches that his Mother is to be adored and venerated as is fitting for the Mother of God." This cannot be *latria*. As Mother, Mary was also "handmaiden; and the person of the Mother is infinitely inferior to the Person of the Son" (ad 4). Hence, "according to the law of justice and the proper order," adoration of, and love for, Mary should be infinitely below those that are due to the Son.

Further light is thrown on the cult of Mary by Bonaventure's treatment of the cult of the Cross (q. 4) and of the "members of Christ," who are the saints (q. 5).

Bonaventure is acquainted both with a general cult of crucifixes and with a special cult of the true Cross. The question asked concerns the *crux Christi*, the true Cross and its relics. Bonaventure refutes the claim of a cult of *hyperdulia* for the Cross. Any kind of *adoratio*, as he says (and *hyperdulia* is one kind), is first of all prayer, *oratio*; and prayer, like *allocutio*, can be addressed only to intelligent beings. "*Adoratio* is a certain *oratio* directed to something; whence to adore is to pray for something" (*Adorare est ad aliquid orare*: undoubtedly an unscientific etymology: *ad . . . orare!*). Yet Bonaventure also rejects the conclusion of others, that adoration of *latria* is correct since it is referred to the one who hung on the Cross. Discussing a passage from John of Damascus (*De fide orthodoxa*, ch. 16), Bonaventure admits that the traditional veneration of the true Cross is offered to it "not as a thing but as a sign." Yet the true Cross is also, for the Damascene (ch. 11), more than a sign. It is venerated too "by reason of its material . . . because one should venerate not only the form but also the true wood of the Cross from which the Lord hung. In other crosses only the form is to be venerated, not the material." Furthermore, the liturgy includes a solemnity for "the Invention and the Exaltation of the Cross," which is similar to the "feasts of the saints." Where the cult of Mary includes *latria* for Christ and *hyperdulia* for her, the cult of the true Cross has two aspects. These are *latria* for Christ, and reverence for the wood: "and this is an honor of veneration." The wood of the Cross has a certain similarity to the sacraments, which are venerated as containing "somehow the causality of our salvation."

Indeed, the Cross is a mere creature. It is not adored as a thing, but as a *signum rememorativum* leading to the Crucified as an image of what it shows (ad 1). Unlike the Virgin, who can be addressed directly since she is endowed with intelligence, the Cross receives no adoration in itself: "when we adore it, we intend to plead with the Crucified, not with his sign" (ad 2). Heaven and earth lead to God "according to the general way in which a creature leads to the Creator." The Cross, however, is unique; it is in some way a "most special memorial of the Crucified" (ad 3). Praises are of two kinds. Unlike the praise of virtue, the praise of beauty pays no attention to merit. Both kinds are included in the adoration of the Cross. First, honor is extended to it on account of the Crucified, "whose virtue, intelligence, and excellence are above all." Yet honor is also offered to the Cross as such for the "nobility and excellence" it derives from God who "hung from it and liberated humankind." For this reason "the Church sings many praises of it; and by the presence of this most sacred wood many benefits and miracles have been distributed to the faithful" (ad 4).

When, in q. 5, Bonaventure asks about the cult of saints as members of Christ, his answer is brief. Since we are members of Christ according to his human nature, without losing our status as servants, the saints among us cannot receive *latria*: this is due solely to the Creator. "The head is at a greater distance from the body by reason of the divinity with which it is one." The answers to objections, however, raise important points on the cult of angels.

Did Abraham, in Gen 18, adore three angels? One may assume here that Bonaventure was acquainted with the traditional iconography of both East and West, showing the three divine Persons under the image of the three angels who visited the patriarch under the oaks of Mamre. These were, for the Seraphic Doctor, "angels and rational creatures," who had the special mission of representing the Trinity. Abraham therefore offered them an honor of *dulia* as to creatures, but also a cult of *latria*, "not to the sign but to the Signified" (ad 1). Yet, if angels were objects of *dulia* in the Old Testament, it is not so in the New; no cult of angels is now allowed. As a proof of this, we read that the angel, in Rv 19:10, refused to be adored by John, even though John intended only a cult of *dulia*. Bonaventure finds three reasons for this refusal: first, John was himself of a higher dignity than many angels; second, people could have mistakenly concluded from *dulia* that *latria* was also appropriate; third—this being a special reason proposed by Gregory (In Ev Jn I, hom. 8, n. 2)—"humankind was raised through Christ above the angelic nature." Hence what was permissible under the Old Covenant has been abolished by the New: "After the glorification of the human nature in Christ, the angels do not tolerate that this nature be subjected to them, which they see seated at the right hand of the Father" (ad 2).

Though somewhat peripheral to our topic, q. 6, about the cult of the Devil, which is a form of idolatry, raises the problem of supernatural apparitions. It is not permissible, for Bonaventure, to adore the Devil with *latria* even if he has put on the external appearance of Christ. In such a case, "ignorance provides no excuse." For three ways are commonly available to test the truth of apparitions. The first is to heed the warning of Scripture that "many will come mendaciously in the name of Christ." The second is "the remedy of internal prayer, by which one must have recourse to God for the enlightenment of one's heart." The third is the "suspense of one's credulity," in keeping with the scriptural injunction to test the spirits if they be of God (1 Jn 4:1). Such apparitions therefore are "more to be feared than to be desired." And Bonaventure tells the story of a certain St Peter, a desert father, who, faced with an apparition that seemed to be of Christ, though it was in fact the Devil, closed his eyes and said that he did not wish to see Christ in this life. "On the contrary, there are accounts of several persons who believed themselves and desired to be worthy of visions, and who fell into many insanities and errors."

* * * * *

Bonaventure's operative category in determining what kind of cult may be due to Christ, to Mary, and to saints in general, is the category of "sign." Cult, in the full sense of worship, is addressed only to God. Everything human, including the humanity of Christ, can receive worship only insofar as, as a sign, it so points to God that worship goes, through it, to God. The sign keeps nothing for itself. It acts as a pointer or as a channel. The most appropriate sign leading to God is the humanity of Christ, since it belongs to the divine Word incarnate. The icons of Christ follow, pointing, not to themselves as pictures or works of art, but to the divine Person whom they signify. The Cross of Jesus, as the historical instrument of the Passion, comes next in rank, leading directly to the crucified Lord. The Virgin Mary and the saints can come only after those more immediate signs of the divine dimension in Christ. For the signs that are only signs keep nothing for themselves of the honor that is offered them: all honor is passed on to the model or archetype whom they signify, namely, to Christ in his divinity. But the signs who are also persons in their own right, like the Virgin and the saints, do not transmit to Christ all the honor they receive, for some of this honor properly pertains to them as persons. The cult of *latria* must go to God only. Yet the saints, including the Virgin, receive in their own name a cult of *dulia*, or deep respect and veneration, on account of their life and the holiness which they exemplify. Because of Mary's nearness to her divine Son, however, she receives *hyperdulia*. That is, the honor addressed to her goes first of all to her Son: she acts as a sign directing her devotees to the Incarnation. And whatever honor goes to her own person is addressed to her in thanksgiving for the great actions that God performed in and through her.

Bonaventure's theology is in fact—another interesting point in our ecumenical age—closer to that of Orthodox theology and piety than the more common Western tradition: the icons as such are channels of grace and not only reminders of Jesus or substitutes for the written Scriptures. They have an integrity of their own as sacramental means of worship. The divine presence shines through them for those who approach them in faith. The world is filled with the divine presence of the Word; and this presence comes to us through the saints, living icons of God, as well as through the pictures and paintings which, as providential signs, bring our prayer and adoration to the eternal model and archetype of all, the divine Word.

Notes

1. *Comm. on the Sentences,* III, d. 8, a. 1, q. 1, ad 4.

2. d. 9, a. 1, q. 4.

3. d. 9, a. 1, q. 1.

4. On Bonaventure's later position on this matter, see below, ch. 10.

CHAPTER 7

PRINCIPLES OF
MARIAN PREACHING

The celebration of Marian feasts, today as in the thirteenth century, does not follow the chronological order of events in Mary's life. Chronologically, the proper sequence would be: Mary's Nativity, the Annunciation (if this is considered a Marian feast, which is not the case in our contemporary calendar), the Purification, and the Assumption. What was actually celebrated in Bonaventure's time followed another sequence: Purification (February 2), Annunciation (March 25), Assumption (August 15) and Nativity (September 8). The two events recorded in Scripture came first, the two that are unbiblical came later. This discrepancy between history and liturgy derives from the difference between basic biblical devotion and the impact of theological developments upon liturgical prayer.

It also illustrates a difference between the festivals of Christ and those of Mary. In Christ and his feasts, the Church celebrates an event with ascertainable historical dimensions, the Incarnation. In commemorating Mary, the Forthbringer of God, the Church solemnizes theological insights into the fulness of the Incarnation: the Word was made flesh, not of some "eternal woman" of imagination, but of one particular Palestinian Jewish woman. In so doing, however, he enlarged the scope of her life to the universal dimension of his own mission. She became the medium of his task as Redeemer. We are therefore to expect, in the homiletic encomium of Mary's feasts, a blend of down to earth realism, stressing the reality of the Incarnation, and flights of fancy, in which the preacher extols the paradoxical uniqueness of the role of this woman as the Mother of the Lord. Yet, in the thirteenth century, this extolling was not done haphazard. It followed certain general rules, which the present chapter will investigate.

* * * * *

Bonaventure's homilies on the Virgin Mary are built on what may be called the metaphorical principle: the teachings of the Scriptures are done, not only by the words, sentences, and ideas expressed in their written language, but also by the metaphorical dimension of the things or events described in this language. This is primarily a Christological principle: "Because the mystery of the Incarnation of the Lord is so hidden and profound that no intellect can catch it, no tongue explain it, the Holy Spirit, condescending to human infirmity, decided to suggest it with numerous metaphors, guided by which we would come to some awareness of it."[1] Rather than an analytical enquiry into grammar and meaning, or an historical determination of the natural and human events described—that is, of what Bonaventure has elsewhere identified as the literal sense of Scripture—the interpreter should, with the help of divine grace, strive for an insight into the spiritual dimensions of the images and comparisons which abound in Scripture. The principle is extended to the Virgin Mary, since she herself pertains to the mystery of the Incarnation.

For Mary as for Christ, the metaphorical principle, which expresses the divine intention in regard to the meaning of Scripture, justifies a metaphorical method of reading the texts. In both cases, however, the method is liable to two opposite risks. On the one hand, there will be those who will deny certain applications and interpretations of the biblical metaphors. Bonaventure remarks as much: "The solemnity of the present day, which is that of the Purification of Mary, is explained with these words taken from Malachi [3:3]; if they are superficially considered, there is no connection of the word with the feast, and the assumed prophecy seems to be absurd."[2] On the other hand, a sort of inflation on the interpreter's part is possible, so that one metaphor, or, as Bonaventure also says, one "parabolical similitude," will gain more persuasive power from a second one, and then from a third, as though a multiplicity of metaphors were able to compensate for the weakness of each of them.

Bonaventure, however, attributes the multiplicity of metaphors in the first place to the Holy Spirit, and finds a justification for it in the depth of the mysteries. He expresses this in a major passage, in which he applies directly to the Virgin Mary the metaphorical principle at work in the revelation of Christ and of the Incarnation:

Such is the excellence of the glorious Virgin that all tongues, Scriptures, prophecies, and parabolical similitudes fall short of the proper narrative and praise of her. Whence the Holy Spirit, through the prophets' mouths, commends her not only with words but also with images and parabolical similitudes; and since no parabolical similitude perfectly suffices to express her excellence, therefore manifold similitudes and metaphors are introduced into her praise. Sometimes, metaphorical similitudes are introduced into her praise from lower nature, as for instance the similitude of the root, the earth, and the stick; sometimes, from intermediate nature, as that of the source, the cloud, and the mist; sometimes, from supercelestial nature, as the metaphor of the sun, the moon, and the star. Among all the metaphorical similitudes the most excellent seems to be the metaphorical similitude taken from the sun. For the solar body is the most excellent of all the material bodies, and because of its excellence it designates, above all, Jesus Christ. Since, however, what belongs to the head is referred to the head and members, and the most excellent of the members of Christ is the blessed Virgin, it is proper enough to compare her to the sun. . . .[3]

This explanation implies what modern authors may call a Christotypical basis for Mariology: images which apply primarily to Christ the head may be applied secondarily to Mary as the first and most excellent member of his body. Yet this is not the main point of the text. On the one hand, to see Mary as a member, be it the best one, of the body of Christ, amounts to using an ecclesiotypical principle: what is generally true of the Church is more particularly and excellently true of the Virgin Mary. On the other, the central point of the text is that, in the area where the teachings and doctrines about Christ carry implications regarding the *Ecclesia* and its members, a metaphorical theology is proper. What is not expressed explicitly may be implicitly hinted at. But the passage from implicit to explicit is not to be done by human logic: it was done by the Spirit himself in the inspiring of the biblical writers. It is embodied in the text in a spiritual dimension which is open only to those who read it in the Spirit. In other words, there can be no strict rule of spiritual exegesis. The remedy to all defective readings and interpretations is reliance, not on oneself, but on the Holy Spirit. For "the Holy Spirit scrutinizes the things of nought from a higher point of view; and thus, if they are scrutinized spiritually, they seem to have a connection with the present solemnity."[4]

The same general principle and method are formulated more briefly:

> My dear ones, the sublime excellence of the glorious Virgin so far transcends the human capacity that words do not suffice to explain it; and therefore the Holy Spirit, who filled her with the charisms of the virtues, the same Holy Spirit, speaking through the prophets and other doctors of the sacred Scripture, praises her in manifold way, not only through express words, but also through images and metaphors.[5]

Yet the praise of Mary does not belong to the realm of

pure imagination, without a basis in reality. The spiritual sense cannot be invented; it is to be discovered. The metaphorical or parabolical similitudes, the images or figures that lead to it are not fanciful exaggerations. On the contrary, all human language fails:

> We assume at the start that whatever praise is spoken of the blessed Virgin is not said hyperbolically but defectively, in keeping with this word of St Jerome: "Whatever can be said with human words falls short of the praise of God."[6]

Again, a modern reader may be tempted to equate this with a principle which, though it goes back to St Bernard, has been commonly associated with the Mariology of the eighteenth and nineteenth centuries: *de Maria nunquam satis;* one never says enough of the Virgin Mary. The mystery always escapes the words we use to express it. Yet this can be understood in two ways. In the first place— but this is not Bonaventure's meaning—we should always say more than we already say about the virtues and glories of the Virgin Mary. In the second place—and this is Bonaventure's and Jerome's intention—what we say of her, just like what theology is able to formulate of any one of the revealed mysteries, always falls short of the reality. Language fails before the greatness of God's works. Like the divine being, the divine action is ineffable, no less in what touches the Mother of Christ than in the working out of the divine plan for creation and redemption.

* * * * *

It does not follow that Marian exegesis of the Scriptures,

as illustrated in Bonaventure's homilies, is never focussed on the literal and historical sense; nor that the Marian content discovered in the spiritual senses is always located at the same level of these. Bonaventure's exegesis in his homilies is of course not unlike that of his commentaries on Scripture. It does explore the spiritual dimension of the text as it relates to faith (allegory), love (tropology), and hope (anagogy), more than is done in the biblical commentaries. Admittedly, Bonaventure often does in preaching what he would not tolerate in formal exegetical commentary: he frequently starts his explanation directly with one of the spiritual senses that he recognizes in the Bible, without previously explaining the literal meaning. What would not be acceptable in a work of exegesis may be appropriate in a homily. For if the primary purpose of exegesis is knowledge, that of preaching is edification.

Besides, Bonaventure's chief commentaries were made on books of the New Testament: the Gospels of Luke and of John. And, as is explained in the Commentary on the Sentences, the literal meaning of the New Testament—the Gospel—is in itself spiritual; it is also the spiritual meaning of the Old Testament.[7] Therefore, when Bonaventure draws spiritual senses out of the New Testament, he is primarily concerned with applications of the text to faith, love, and hope. When he explores the spiritual senses he has found in the Old Testament, he does something quite different: he searches for anticipations of the mystery of Christ. Such anticipations are seldom apparent at the level of the letter. They emerge from associations and similarities of all kinds between the texts and events of the Old Testament and the texts and realities of the New.

In fact, the fourth homily on the Annunciation places

the Marian meaning directly and entirely at the level of the literal sense, even though this is taken from *Ecclesiasticus*, 24:12: "He who created me took his rest in my tent":

> According to spiritual understandings this can congruently enough fit several [realities]; for according to the literal understanding it fits the Virgin Mary, in whose tent the Lord rested bodily; according to the allegorical one it fits the Church militant, in whose tent the Lord has rested sacramentally; according to the moral one it fits the faithful soul, in whose tent the Lord rests spiritually; according to the anagogical one it fits the heavenly court, in whose tent he rests eternally; and thus what is said, "He who created me took his rest in my tent," is true in every way, namely, literally, allegorically, morally, and anagogically.[8]

The third homily on the Purification features another problematic as it explores the symbolism of the Temple: this is, literally, "the material basilica" of Jerusalem; allegorically, "the virginal womb"; tropologically, "the faithful soul"; anagogically, the "heavenly Jerusalem."[9] Jesus comes to all three to find his rest in them. In the fourth homily for the Nativity of the Virgin, devoted to the symbolism of the Ark of the Covenant in *Apocalypse* 11:19, Bonaventure opens still another perspective: besides the four usual senses, equated, literally, with the actual ark made of "wood and gold," allegorically, with "Christ and the Church," tropologically, with "the episcopate and the holy soul," anagogically, with "the heavenly secret and the Jerusalem on high," he discovers a fifth meaning, which he calls "mystical."[10] This is obtained by gathering together into one the three previous spiritual senses: it is the Virgin Mary:

> Between all the sacred and secret images that are given and instituted by the Lord in the Law of the Image [i.e., the Old Testament], the Ark of the Lord's Covenant is ordered as the most worthy of honor; and this was done, not casually or irrationally, but in keeping with the disposition of the highest Wisdom, which made the Law. For this was not done for the ark because it was crafted out of wood and gold, but because it most aptly prefigured the secrets of God according to the dictate of eternal art. Hence, among the other images which, according to God's manifold wisdom, are sources of meaning, the Ark of the Covenant is filled with a multitude of mystical understandings, so that there is nothing in it which does not lead to some spiritual meaning.

After specifying the three usual spiritual senses, Bonaventure adds: "According to the mystical meaning gathered from all that has been said, it represents the glorious Virgin, the most blessed Mother of God and our Lady, the holy Mary." Bonaventure then elaborates on this mystical meaning in the light of four points of view: "in regard to the material, the content, the efficacy, and the dignity" of the Ark, or, in other words, in regard to "what it is, what it has, what it does, what it receives," or also "according to what it *itself* is, what is *in* it, what is *from* it, and what is *for* it." From all these vantage points, the

Scriptures present abundant evidence which applies directly to the Virgin Mary. "In her life and her conception," she "was not corrupted by the corruption of actual concupiscence; in dying and expiring she was not corrupted by the pain of ashes and worms"; but she had "perfect virtue and deep humility, . . . honest conversation, . . . the fulness of total honesty, which made the Virgin Mary beautiful inside and outside, . . . the quadrangle made of the equality of the fourfold virtue." As to content, "the blessed Mary was the Ark containing manna in the suavity of grace, the stick in the virtue of faith, the Law in the correctness of her understanding; and she supported the two cherubim in her fulness of wisdom. . . ." As to what she does, Mary "leads the perfect" through "the beginning, the progress, and the evening" of the present life; she "protects those who struggle," and "reconciles the penitents." As to what is for her, the glorious Virgin receives "honor and reverence" in "unanimous, . . . humble, . . . solemn, . . . and untiring veneration."

* * * * *

As this brief analysis shows, Bonaventure's Marian homilies, if they generally follow one method of spiritual exegesis, do not use a universal grid applicable to all texts, images, metaphors, and parabolical similitudes. They endeavor in a variety of ways to explore contrasts and relationships between the Old and the New. The New is always centered Christologically and ecclesiologically, since Mary is always seen in the light of Christ and the Church.

Notes

1. Homilies on the Annunciation, I, (vol. IX, p. 708). In the present study I will use only Bonaventure's sermons for the feasts of Mary; several others, however, also allude to the Virgin, as, for instance, the sermon for Sunday in the octave of the Epiphany, Guy Bougerol, *Sti Bonaventurae Sermones Dominicales*, (Grottaferrata: Collegio S. Bonaventura, 1977), p. 178-185.

2. On the Purification, I (p. 626). My references for the homilies on the feasts of Mary are to the BAC edition, vol. IV, Madrid, 1947.

3. On the Nativity of Mary, II. (p. 911-912).

4. On the Purification, I (p. 626).

5. On the Assumption, IV (p. 880).

6. On the Assumption, III (p. 870).

7. See *Transiency and Permanence*, p. 43-50.

8. On the Annunciation, IV (p. 772).

9. On the Purification, III, (p. 690).

10. On the Nativity, IV (p. 932-950).

CHAPTER 8

THE FOUR FEASTS
OF MARY

As it was suggested at the beginning of the last chapter, the feasts of Mary were not as numerous in the liturgical calendar known to Bonaventure as in ours. The feast of Mary's Conception, practiced in certain places, was not yet universal; and it was rejected, for the reasons we have already seen, by Bonaventure as it was by Thomas Aquinas and as it had been by St Bernard. Bonaventure's Marian preaching took place chiefly on the occasion of the four feasts of the Purification, the Annunciation, the Assumption, and the Nativity of Mary. Some other sermons of course spoke also of the Virgin Mary, though seldom as their main theme. In this chapter, we will concentrate on the sermons preached for Mary's feasts.

Among Bonaventure's homilies that have been preserved, five were preached for the Purification, six for the Annunciation, five for the Assumption, and six for the Nativity. Some are quite short, others much longer. A few have little originality, being repetitions of what Bonaventure had already said in another sermon. Several have a double feature, in keeping with the rules of the university of Paris. A professor of theology had the obligation, on certain days, of preaching. The rule required that the preacher of the morning would preach again in the evening: to the morning *sermo* there then corresponds an evening *collatio* or conference. Bonaventure often used the *collatio* to complete what he had said in the morning, developing another point, which had usually been announced, but not treated, in the sermon at Mass.

In this chapter we will follow the liturgical order and draw attention to a number of themes or major ideas that are featured in Bonaventure's Marian homilies. In doing so, we naturally should keep in mind the principles of Marian preaching and the double aspect that ensues. On the one hand, Mary's historical reference derives entirely from the available data concerning her son Jesus. On the other, her own place in the worshipping mind is more at the level of poetry than it is at that of history.

* * * * *

Bonaventure's homiletical method stresses certain main lines of imagery and thought. While each of the four feasts of Mary is itself approached from diverse angles, each one seems to bear an accent of its own. The feast of the Purification, which records a biblical event, demonstrates that, like Jesus himself, Mary submitted to the Law by superfluous and generous obedience. For she already belonged to the new Law and was exempt from the regulations and restrictions of the Old. Images help to understand Mary, yet, by God's very special grace, she herself had passed, in her life on earth, from shadows and images to the reality. Her Purification therefore presents fruitful lessons for the Church, which in some way succeeded the church of the Old Testament, in another was something quite new. The image of the Church and its hierarchy constitutes in fact the guiding thread of the homilies on Mary's Purification. In the first, Mary is a model for the "hierarchies," including the ecclesial hierarchy. The second homily sees her as *Liberatrix* of the faithful, in both their purification (morning sermon) and their sanctification (evening *collatio*). The third homily explores the symbol of the Temple, which Mary is in her own body.

For the feast of the Annunciation, which of course is also biblical, the coming of the angel and his message to the Virgin hold a prominent place only in the fifth homily. In all of them, it is the theme of holiness, in its nature and its process, which is predominant. In the first homily Mary is the one who "leads by the hand" those who are willing to follow her. The second homily analyzes her virginity in itself and in its fecundity, especially in relation to the seven gifts of the Holy Spirit. The third homily shows that the image of Mary throws light on the fruits of the Incarnation "under the metaphor of the fecund earth": in God's gift and Mary's reception of it (morning sermon), and in the ensuing fruits of it for the faithful (evening *collatio*). In the fourth homily, Mary is the literal embodiment of divine wisdom, serving as a model for the Church, the faithful soul, and the heavenly court. The fifth and sixth homilies are devoted to the two parts of the "Hail, Mary": the angelic greeting at the

Annunciation (fifth homily), and Elizabeth's addition to it at the Visitation (sixth homily).

The other two feasts are unbiblical. Yet their treatment is not substantially different from that of the two biblical feasts. The Assumption features, naturally enough, images of ascent. That Mary's life ended through death, like that of everyone else and especially like that of Jesus, has been mentioned in connection with the Purification: in "dying and expiring," the Virgin was not subject to corruption. Yet very little stress is now placed on Mary's being assumed into heaven body and soul after her death. When this is stated, it is called only a pious belief:

> Above all the saints she is said to have been made noble and sublime in regard to the overflowing of her joys, with which she overflowed uniquely above all the saints. For this reason the angels at her assumption were saying: "Who is this one who ascends from the wilderness, overflowing with joys, embracing her beloved"? She overflowed with these joys above the college of the saints, not only in her soul, but also in her own body, which is piously believed and proven to have been glorified in the assumption of her soul.[1]

The Assumption of Mary is therefore first of all the heavenly glorification of her soul; it is also, secondarily, the participation of her body in the glory of heaven. In fact, the homilies on the Assumption insist on the spiritual, not on the corporal, dimension of the feast. Mary is, in the first homily, the "mountain of the house of the Lord." In the second, she is "more beautiful than the sun." The third describes her coming to God and God's welcoming her, with the unexpected and paradoxical idea that God somehow "adored" Mary. The fourth homily sees her as a source that has enlarged into a river and has finally and wonderfully turned into light. In the fifth homily, the spiritual glorification of the Virgin is carefully analyzed.

The feast of Mary's Nativity has a special importance in Bonaventure's theology. For it was in part the existence of this feast—celebrating Mary's holiness at her birth—which led medieval theologians to denounce the feast of her Conception as spurious, since Mary was believed to have been conceived in original sin. Yet her nativity is not recorded in the Scriptures, and the legends about it that were familiar to the Middle Ages derive from gospels that were known to be apocryphal. In fact, very little is said about Mary's birth. The feast serves as an occasion to preach on Mary as being symbolically a light for the faithful (first homily), the rising sun (second), an "admirable vase" artistically fashioned and richly adorned by the Creator (third), and the Ark of the Covenant" (fourth homily).

* * * * *

In these homilies for the Marian festivals and in a few others which, though preached on other occasions, give Mary a prominent place, certain symbols or ideas clearly stand out. The themes of the Temple and of the Ark of the Covenant have already been touched upon. Several others are worth paying attention to. We will survey what Bonaventure says about the name of Mary, about the Virgin and the "hierarchies," about the beauty of the Virgin, and about Mary's relation to God.

The name of Mary

The name of Mary is of special interest to the Seraphic Doctor, who discerns in it a prefiguration of what the Virgin was called to be. It comes in for special attention in the second homily for the Purification. Bonaventure addresses the Virgin in the development of his "pro-theme." This is the introduction which, in the sacred rhetoric of the scholastic period, preceded a solemn homily. After announcing his main text, with which the bulk of the sermon will deal, the preacher announced a second text, the "protheme." A brief explanation of this second text helped him to begin his development on the main text; it often afforded the occasion to summarize the main idea to be developed; and it usually led the preacher to invite his listeners to pray for him, that God may give him the proper words and inspiration. In the present introduction, Bonaventure applies to Mary the words addressed to Judith: "Pray for us, for you are a holy woman" (*Judith* 8:24):

> You, glorious Virgin, who are called Mary, that is, Star of the Sea; who are called Mary, that is, Bitter Sea; who are called Mary, that is, Lady, pray for us who are to be illuminated, purified, and perfected. Because you are the Star of the Sea, pray for us who are to be illuminated; because you are a Bitter Sea, which supports no corruption, pray for us who are to be purified; because you are Lady, pray for us who are to be perfected. These three we need in

order that the efficacy of the divine Speech (*sermo*) be in us, since the divine Speech is ordered to the illumination of our intellect, the purification of our affection, the perfection of our work or effectiveness. And this we cannot do without the glorious Virgin's intervention; let us therefore pray to her. . . .[2]

Of the three meanings of the name of Mary, the central one is Star of the Sea. Mary is the "star that rises in Jacob" according to *Numbers* 24:17. Besides, in the appellation, Star of the Sea, the other two meanings of the name are implied. This is stated in the first homily for the Purification: "The principal interpretation of 'Mary' is Star of the Sea, and this interpretation comprises all the others."[3] After quoting St Bernard Bonaventure goes on: "The glorious Virgin is the Star of the Sea, purifying those who are in the sea of this world, illuminating and perfecting them. Let us therefore follow the Star of the Sea who purifies through the weeping of *bitter* compunction, the Star of the Sea who illuminates through application of the illuminative power, the Star of the Sea who perfects through the vow of perfection." This passage asserts also: "She is the purifier, the illuminator, and the perfector. I am mistaken unless the name of the Virgin implies all three. For Mary is interpreted as Bitter Sea, *Illuminatrix*, and Lady; she received the graces of purgation, illumination, and perfection," which the text relates to her sorrows, her lights, and her perfection.

Indeed, Bonaventure's etymological conclusions are of little standing in our age of scientific linguistics. The really interesting point, however, is that his interpretation of the name of Mary helps him to connect her with a favorite topic of all his writings, the theme of the "hierarchies."

The "Hierarchies"

The notion of "hierarchy" came to the Scholastics from the several Latin translations of the works of Denys, who was identified with Denys the Areopagite, converted by Paul in Athens according to the book of Acts. Briefly, Denys saw a proportional analogy between the divine hierarchy of the Holy Trinity, the heavenly hierarchy of the angels, which he subdivided into three triads at three levels of descending dignity (Seraphim, Cherubim, and Thrones; Dominations, Virtues, and Powers; Principalities, Archangels, and Angels), and with the hierarchy of the Church, itself divided into the two triads of the priests (bishops, priests, and liturgists) and the initiates (monks, holy laity, and catechumens). Denys, however, did not see these hierarchies as merely institutional structures: they are spiritual. For the process of descent is one of illumination or influence of the lower by the higher orders. And this influence was brought down to the three acts of purification, illumination, and perfection or union.

Bonaventure made considerable use of these ideas in his analysis of the spiritual life. This was the topic of a special writing, the *Triple Way* (*De Triplici Via*). Unlike most interpreters, however, the Seraphic Doctor understood the "three hierarchic acts" of purification, illumination, and union, to be parallel or simultaneous rather than successive. The soul's ascent to God passes through the three ways of constant purification from sin, progressive illumination by divine grace, and growing union with God who makes himself the soul's heavenly Spouse.

This is precisely the key to much of what we may now call Bonaventure's spiritual Mariology. Already the explanation of the name of Mary as Star of the Sea has brought in the notion of the hierarchic acts: these are the actions that are typical of each of the three ways, purification, illumination, and union. Mary has been asked to pray for us, who still need to be purified, illuminated, and perfected. The remainder of the homily, including the evening *collatio*, expounds the principle: in Mary we find a model for our own sanctification. "By the word, sanctification, we understand the very sanctification and purification which we have conceived, thanks to the oblation of her Son and the purification of the Virgin."[4] The Son's oblation or sacrifice is explained in the second part of the *collatio*. Up to that point, Bonaventure explores at length how the Virgin's purification is a model for that of the saints (possibly *the* model, but since the Latin language uses no definite or indefinite article it is difficult to decide which it should be!). The Virgin wished to be purified, "not because she was unclean, not because she was subject to the Law, but in order to be the form of sanctification and purification." The notion of "form" has an extrinsic denotation: it is a model visible to others; it also has the intrinsic meaning of interior beauty. The form, in Aristotle's philosophy, shapes the beauty of the matter it informs. In line with this, it was fitting that Mary "present the form of sanctification as the saint of saints, *Panagia* in Greek, ... And see that whatever was in her was the form and exemplar of sanctification in others":

There was in her the pure receptacle of all sanctification by virtue of the fulness of divine grace; there was the clear mirror of all sanctification by virtue of the graciousness of her conversation; there was in her, thirdly, the radiating principle of all sanctification by virtue of the conception of the Son of God; there was also, fourthly, the exemplar, to be imitated, of all sanctification by virtue of the fame of her purification. And if she had the first three, it was proper that she also have the fourth.

Because of her task as the Forthbringer of God, Mary was sanctified by the Holy Spirit, "not only in what she was as a person, but also in what she was as a nature, for she had sanctification not only for and in herself, but because she had to be the principle of another by generation, so that what was to be procreated from her would be born holy; and by that which was born from her all are sanctified." This distinction between holiness as person and holiness as nature is unusual. Yet its import is clear: Mary's personal holiness affected herself; her holiness in her purified nature affected the human nature of Jesus, to which she contributed bodily.

The rest of this Homily II on purification amounts to a treatise on the spiritual life, as Bonaventure answers the question: "But how should we come spiritually to the temple"? The path is the threefold way of purification, illumination, and union. Bonaventure, however, uses a less scholastic vocabulary at this point. Purification is the indwelling of the divine Majesty in the soul through the fear of God; illumination is the indwelling of the divine Wisdom through knowledge of the truth; union is the indwelling of "God as Goodness" through the sanctification of love. This in turn demands the sanctification of external actions and behavior, for "our body is a vase, since it is the vase of the soul, insofar as it is its matter and the receptacle of the Holy Spirit by grace." Therefore,

> this soul is God's holy temple, when God as Majesty indwells its capacity to act, when God as Wisdom indwells its capacity to know, when God as Goodness indwells its capacity to love, when God as Holiness indwells its capacity to minister. Of all these we have the example in the glorious Virgin. . . .

That Mary is such a model of hierarchic action implies that she has been placed not only above her fellow human beings who are in the process of being purified, illuminated, and perfected, but even above the angels who, as Denys sees the universe—and the Seraphic Doctor still shares his vision—nurture the purification, illumination, and perfection of humankind. Indeed, this is the meaning of her Assumption: "She has been raised above the angelic hierarchy which purifies, illumines, and perfects, and above the human hierarchy to be purified, illuminated, and perfected."[5] To this elevation Bonaventure devotes his first homily on the Assumption of Mary. Significantly, the name of Mary is again connected with this: "The Virgin performs this act [of hierarchic influence] in the hierarchies of angels and men, that are below her. Whence Mary is fittingly called Bitter Sea, since she purifies; *Illuminatrix*, since she illuminates; Lady, since she brings to perfection and consummation."

Bonaventure reads this in *Apocalypse* 12:1: "A great

sign appeared in the sky: A woman clothed with the sun" . . .:

> This woman is the royal Virgin, who is said to be "clothed with the sun," that is, with the beauty of the Sun of Justice; "and the moon under her feet," that is, the glory of the world, strenuously despised, which is at times waning or waxing; "and on her head a crown of twelve stars," that is, all the honor and dignity, the glory and sublimity, and the nobility of kind, that have been granted the twelve orders of the saints designated by the twelve shining stars, of which nine are those of the heavenly spirits, and three are of the threefold state of men, the active, the contemplative, and the prelates. For whatever dignity and glory have been given them partially have been integrally conceded to the holy Virgin.[6]

Mary and the Church

The superiority of the Virgin over all created hierarchies in heaven and on earth determines her basic relation to the church militant. If indeed, in Bonaventure's perspective, Mary has been raised by God, from the early time of her life, above all created hierarchies, then it is legitimate to find in her the image, form, or figure of the divine plan for the world. Mary may then be called "the Empress of every creature."[7] She is "the *Liberatrix* of all humankind,"[8] "the mountain of God,"[9] on which the house of God, which is the Church, has been built, and which the faithful are ascending; she is "the mother of all the saints";[10] she is "the gate of our salvation,"[11] and therefore also "our mother."[12] In her God-given transcendence she is to be imitated from afar; and, in keeping with the Dionysian theory on the hierarchies, she is also a source or channel of inspiration and grace. Under the metaphor of the Sun, Mary "illuminates the whole Church and the machine of the world."[13] She is "the spiritual Sun of the world." Her image will therefore throw light on the church militant.

Bonaventure devotes special attention to the Church's hierarchy in the more popular sense of the term. This is the sacerdotal triad of bishops, priests, and liturgists (or ministers of the lower orders). It corresponds to what more recent nomenclature often calls the "magisterium." Indeed, the Church is built on solid foundations:

> The Church draws its origin from the blessed Virgin by faith; its altitude, by hope; its stability, by charity. Whence she [Mary] is the mountain of the house of God; it has to be built on these three, which were powerful in the saints: in the patriarchs, faith; in the prophets, hope; in the apostles, charity, though all three are in all of them. Whence they are themselves called mountains and foundations of the house of the Church. . . . At the summit of all of them, the blessed Virgin is called a "prepared mountain," because whatever has been promised or revealed in them has been completed in her; and whatever grace flowed into them derived from her and through her.[14]

Yet Bonaventure exhibits no great admiration for the magisterium as it is and functions. "Prelates," that is, bishops, "should be such mountains."[15] Yet there are some who "corrupt and scandalize by bad example." Instead of being "radiant," and even, like the Mother of Christ, "deiform," some are "dark mountains": they teach "false dogmas against the truth of holy Scripture, false counsels against the examples of the saints, false judgments against the decrees of the Fathers and the rule of the Laws." We should all be "such that divine grace descends into us and is channelled to others through us." Yet some of us are "proud, envious, undevout." It is characteristic of clerics that "they seek the leaves of words and do not bear the fruits of good works."[16] "One should cry today because the ministers of the tabernacle, who should set the example of purity and should sanctify the people, pollute and bring ugliness."[17]

By contrast, in relation to what ministers should be, the Virgin "is the regulatory exemplar of the ecclesial hierarchy, and therefore is she called the Star of the Sea."[18] She is, among other things, the model of penance:

> I say first that the purification of the glorious Virgin signifies the purification of the ecclesial hierarchy. . . . I say therefore that, in order to begin the purification of the Church's ministers, the glorious Virgin was purified interiorly and in truth by receiving sanctifying grace.[19]

This contains suitable teaching about baptism as the taking away of original sin. "But since the ecclesial hierarchy often suffers damage in its members, it needs to be restored by divine grace, and another sanctifying grace is necessary, namely, the penitential grace." This is imaged in Mary's Purification in the Temple after "forty days." Forty is both "the number of transgression and the number of penance." For in sin there is a quadrilateral made of "suggestion, delectation, consent, and action. Multiply this quadrilateral by ten and you have forty; multiply transgression, suggestion, consent, and delectation, insofar as they are opposed to the divine law, you have the number ten [i.e., from the ten commandments] multiplied by four, and thus you have forty." Likewise, forty is the number of penance: it is obtained by multiplying recognition of sin, detestation of it, accusation, and emendation, by the ten commandments. This number forty, which thus designates "the integrity of penance, is in Mary, not for herself, but for the Church." Moses fasted forty days before receiving the Law; Elijah fasted forty days before coming to "a secret colloquy with God"; and Jesus fasted forty days and nights before he began his ministry. These are the "legal, prophetic, and evangelical purifications; and all these are signified by the Purification of Mary." The three of them should be found in the Church, for "the first is only purificative; the second is purificative and illuminative; the third is purificative, illuminative, and perfective." Bonaventure thus brings back the theme of the threefold way, and the assertion of Mary's standing above all hierarchy: "She has in herself the entire beauty of the ecclesial hierarchy; and she is today the beauty of the heavenly hierarchy."

What is thus affirmed of Mary's image in relation to the purity of the magisterium should also be said of the other ecclesial hierarchy of Denys, made of monks, laity, catechumens. To them, though chiefly to the friars of his own order, were most of Bonaventure's homilies addressed. To them the Seraphic Doctor enjoined:

"Acknowledge the virginity by which God is your Father, and how you have been conceived of the Holy Spirit, your Mother is the glorious Virgin, and your heritage, the kingdom of heaven."[20] It is for all the members of the Church that Mary, the model of the three ways, functions as *Purgatrix, Illuminatrix, Perfectrix*, "the exemplar and the form of all spiritual sanctifications."[21] She is "the Mother of Solomon,"[22] the "Queen of mercy."[23]

Bonaventure believes that a warm piety toward the Virgin is indispensable to holiness: "I have never read about any of the saints, who would have no special devotion to the glorious Virgin."[24] Accordingly, his fifth homily on the Annunciation, commenting on the archangel's message, repeats like a refrain: "Let us therefore say with the Angel: Hail, full of grace."[25] As the sixth homily comments on the sequel in the Visitation: "and blessed is the fruit of your womb," we are given here another hint that Bonaventure was acquainted with some form of the rosary.

Be that as it may, Bonaventure recommends, as a mode of Marian devotion, the contemplation of Mary's beauty. This is implied in the frequent metaphor of the light: Mary herself is a light; she is "the light of the sun."[26] Already is she "great river,"[27] a "supersplendid river," as Bonaventure says with a very Italian fondness for superlatives. She who was a source, and grew into a river where "are hidden all the treasures of wisdom and knowledge," has also become light. It is "rare that a source be transformed into light; nor is it the way of nature that an elemental body be transformed into a heavenly one, but this is the way of the Virgin's glorification."[28] Mary radiates beauty, in keeping with the metaphor of the sun:

The sun wonderfully makes the universe beautiful

by its presence and its rising; thus the blessed Virgin adorns the whole world; for she is an admirable vase containing the light, so that, were she removed from the center, the whole universe would be deformed. For if you remove the Mother of God from the world, by the same token you remove the incarnate Word; and once he has been removed, there still remain the deformity of sinners and the error of sins. For the divine Wisdom, Christ, who is the beauty beautifying all things, would be removed.[29]

One may therefore say: "It is delightful enough to see the material sun with our material eyes, but much more joyful is it for faithful eyes to contemplate the very beauty of the Virgin. . . ." Drawing on a different analogy, Bonaventure compares Mary to the earth, which he believes to be located "in the middle of the center of the world, so that all the heavenly bodies directly look at her."[30] In the *collatio* corresponding to this sermon, Bonaventure describes the "fruit of the virginal womb" as being "sublime and delightful, because it is most beautiful to see, . . . most beautiful to see with the eye of faith."[31] Such fruits are "all the saints and the just, but especially Jesus Christ himself. . . ." Mary herself was "gracious and beautiful, not only in her body but also in her soul, . . . beautiful inside and outside."[32] One may apply to her the words that are said of Esther in Scripture: "She was extremely pretty and of incredible beauty; she was seen by the eyes of all as gracious and lovable."

Mary as the bride of God

The theme of the God-given beauty of the Virgin is

harmoniously prolonged in that of her being God's very special spouse. This had been a familiar idea in spiritual literature: the commentaries on the *Song of Songs* commonly read the Old Testament poem as the song of the espousals between God and every faithful soul. The Virgin Mary being seen as the best and highest example of fidelity, she naturally became the first and the most complete bride of God. This union was celebrated at the Annunciation, when the divine Word dwelt in her body: "The Creator of all things took his rest in the tabernacle of her virginal womb, because in it he established a nuptial chamber for himself to become our brother, he prepared a royal throne to be our king, he put on the sacerdotal vestment to be our pontiff."[33] As a result, Mary shared in these three aspects of Christ, becoming "the Mother of all the saints,"[34] and "the Queen of all."[35] Finally, Jesus put on in her the "white and red vestment" of the priesthood, "so that he would not be alone the Advocate, but she also would be, in order that, through two persons whom it is impossible to refute, namely, the Son and the Mother, we have a most solid support."[36] Indeed, "the blessed Virgin, our advocate, cannot not be heard." This makes her more than the nuptial chamber: she is the bride. Like Esther, she "pleased the angels of God and the eyes of the Bridegroom by the greatness of her comeliness and beauty."[37]

This dimension of God's relation to Mary explains Bonaventure's bold language when, in what must be his most adventurous "parabolical similitude," he describes God's coming out toward the Virgin in her Assumption, accompanied by all the heavenly court. Angels, patriarchs, apostles, martyrs are there, along with married and widowed women. Her own sisters hasten to see "their prelate and abbess."[38] The entire Trinity approaches, "even though not locally, yet in favorable influence, highest joy, and deiform glory":

> The entire blessed Trinity has known you, Mary, as bride of chaste love, palace of holy dwelling, instrument of wondrous deed. Or let us say, with distinctions: the Father has known the blessed Mary as the house of his majesty. . . . The Son has recognized her as the principle of his humanity or humility. The Holy Spirit has recognized her as the repository of his goodness.

Yet this is not all: "he adored her." Bonaventure exclaims: "What do you do, Lord? You, the true Lord whom all must adore, you adore a woman? I adore, He says, because two things make her adorable, namely, her motherhood and the merit of her humility." And yet, is this not "against the laws for the Son to adore the Mother"? No indeed, for "Jesus adores, not an ordinary Mother, but a Mother of singular sufficiency, magnificence, and diligence." Because of her humility, in the depth of which she "emptied herself and became nothing, to the point of feeling nothing about herself besides nothing; and therefore God not only exalts her among the saints and raises her above the saints, but corporally adores her in ultimate honor." What does "adore" mean in this context? I would suggest—but in so doing I try to read the mind of Bonaventure in his boldest use of rhetorical similes—that it should be taken in the sense which elsewhere the Seraphic Doctor recognizes to the word, *adoratio*: it is *ad oratio,* "praying to" her. Through the archangel's message, God asked her to accept being the Mother of the Word made flesh. The beginning of the Incarnation was crowned at Mary's Assumption into divine glory: the relationship inaugurated through the angel did not change substantially. God comes to greet her; he still invites her to come, metaphorically "prays" to her, parabolically "adores" her. And Mary's response is still that of her utterly abandoned *fiat.*

Notes

1. On the Assumption, II (p. 862-864); the citation is from the *Song of Songs,* 8, 19.

2. On the Purification, II (p. 656-658).

3. On the Purification, I (p. 639-640).

4. On the Purification, II (p. 658-672).

5. On the Assumption, I (p. 850-851).

6. On the Assumption, II (p. 866).

7. On the Nativity, III (p. 928).

8. On the Purification, II (p. 656).

9. On the Assumption, I (p. 858).

10. On the Annunciation, IV (p. 776).

11. On the Purification, III (p. 698).

12. On the Annunciation, IV (p. 776).

13. On the Nativity, II (p. 920; 924).

14. On the Assumption, I (p. 846).

15. l. c. (p. 847-850).

16. On the Annunciation, V (p. 826).

17. On the Annunciation, IV (p. 782).

18. On the Purification, I (p. 644).

19. On the Purification, I (p. 628-638).

20. l. c. (p. 630); see On the Annunciation, IV (p. 776).

21. On the Purification, II (p. 658).

22. On the Assumption, III (p. 868).

23. On the Annunciation, IV (p. 776).

24. On the Purification, II (p. 662).

25. On the Annunciation, V (p. 800-808).

26. On the Assumption, IV (p. 892).

27. l. c., (p. 888).

28. l. c., (p. 892).

29. On the Nativity, II (p. 914).

30. On the Annunciation, III (p. 760).

31. l. c., *coll.*, (p. 766).

32. On the Annunciation, V (p. 804).

33. On the Annunciation, III, *coll.*, (p. 774).

34. l. c., (p. 776).

35. l. c., (p. 774).

36. On the Annunciation, IV (p. 780).

37. On the Nativity, II (p. 916).

38. On the Assumption, III (p. 870-874).

Part Four

Mystical Insight

CHAPTER 9

THE MYSTIC JOURNEY

As one reads the mystical *opuscula* which Bonaventure composed during his tenure as guardian general of the Franciscan Order, one may be surprised that the Virgin Mary is not prominently featured in the most important of these short works. Yet the reason for this is not far to seek. As we have consistently noted, the Seraphic Doctor's language about the Virgin is always closely related to the methodology that is called for by his immediate purpose. This principle applies to the presence or absence of references to, or of developments about, Mary. However much Bonaventure appears to be carried away by Marian enthusiasm in the metaphorical similes of his sermons, he always remains in control of his methodological tools. Precisely, the method of his basic spiritual writings, the *Pilgrimage of the Soul into God,* his best known work, and the *Threefold Way,* does not call for extensive considerations on the Virgin Mary. This is in part due to a convention of the spiritual authors of the period, who present the mystic journey in a formal, not a psychological, way, set in a well-delineated framework and following a clear map. Variations of the framework, even in the same author, suggest that the heart of the teaching lies in the doctrine and experience corresponding to each stage, not in the structure itself of the journey.

The *Pilgrimage of the Soul into God* was written after Bonaventure had spent some two months (September-October 1259) in the solitude of Mt La Verna, the mountain of Tuscany where Francis of Assisi, in September 1224, had been marked with the stigmata of the passion in the course of an ecstatic experience, the focus of which was the vision of "a winged seraph in the form of the Crucified."[1] Taking this vision as his model, Bonaventure outlines the mystical ascent. Contemplation of the outside world *through* and *in* the traces left by the Creator in all his works leads to contemplation of one's inner world, where to find God *through* the image of himself imprinted in the soul and *in* the same image restored by grace, and thence to a twofold contemplation of the divine name, *through* the oneness of God as Being, and *in* the Trinity of God as the Good. Mary is not formally part of any of these stages of ascent. Yet she appears twice. At the start of the work, in the prologue, Bonaventure prays for enlightenment, invoking "the First Principle" (God the Father), through "his Son, our Lord Jesus Christ, by the intercession of the Virgin Mary, the Forthbringer of the same Jesus Christ, our God and Lord, and of blessed Francis, our leader and father." Mary appears again toward the end of the pilgrimage. For she belongs to the realm of the Incarnation, being associated to the first Cherub of the propitiatory, who is the Word of God born of the Virgin at the fulness of time (chapter 6, n. 5). The last chapter (7) describes the transition of the pilgrim to the heavenly Jerusalem in Christological and Trinitarian terms. Through the work, the operative principle providing the basic pattern has been the image of Francis at Mt La Verna.

The other essential writing on the spiritual life, *The Threefold Way*,[2] was probably written shortly after the *Pilgrimage of the Soul into God*. It analyzes in a very condensed mode the traditional three ways—purgation, illumination, union—which, since the works of Denys, constituted the formal framework of many spiritual itineraries. Here again, the presentation of the purification and illumination of the soul and its union with God require no specific attention to the Virgin. The sermons have admittedly seen her in relation to these three "hierarchic acts," of which she is indeed an outstanding example. She exhibits their fruits in her task as the Forthbringer of God; and these are identified in the *Threefold Way* as peace, truth, and charity. She is also a model for the three levels of prayer in which each way is mapped out, namely, contrition, supplication, adoration. In the process which is thus outlined, Mary is implicitly included, even if she is not specifically mentioned, wherever "the suffrage of the saints" is appealed to or their presence evoked. She is explicitly named at the fourth degree of the "seven degrees that lead to the sleep of peace," where one "shouts in supplication for the fourfold assistance of God the Father, Christ the Redeemer, the Virgin Mary, and the church triumphant."

The Virgin is thus present, in these fundamental works as in all Christian life, where prayer takes place. She is herself in prayer; and her prayer includes the Church militant and all those who, in it, thirst after holiness.

* * * * *

There is a problem of authenticity about some of the spiritual *opuscula* formerly attributed to Bonaventure. Yet this should not interfere very much with our inquiry if we simply leave aside a few spurious or only doubtful pieces.

Among the writings directly destined to the Franciscan Order, the *Rule of Novices*[3] provides a practical starting point. Among the prayers addressed to the Virgin that the novices will say, the anthem, *Salve, Regina,* will be part of the daily liturgical office; but the novices are also invited to recite the *Hail, Mary* in private a number of times: at meals, that is, as Bonaventure says it, "when you drink: after saying *Hail, Mary,* drink with both hands," and mix water with your wine! Every day, between sunrise and sunset, the novices should also recite, "in praise of God and of the blessed Virgin, one hundred *Pater Nosters* with *Gloria Patris,* and as many *Ave Marias* with genuflections." This is undoubtedly the early form of the rosary which was familiar to Bonaventure.

Formal vocal prayers like these, however, find their meaning in the intimate purpose of those who pray. As Bonaventure expresses it in the *Letter containing twenty-five points to remember,*[4] addressed to a Franciscan who must have been a close friend of his, the inner purpose ought to include both love and imitation:

At all times, have for the glorious Queen, the Mother

of our Lord, the highest respectful love; and in all the details and pressures of your needs turn to her as to a very safe shelter; taking her as your advocate, entrust your case, with devotion and confidence, to her who is the Mother of mercy, trying everyday to show her a special and singular veneration. And, that your devotion may be accepted and your veneration agreeable, endeavor with every effort to imitate the traces of her humility and kindness, by cultivating in yourself, with every virtue, in soul and body, the spotless integrity of her purity.

The friars may be assisted in this by the example of St Francis. In the main life of Francis—the *Legenda Major*[5]— which he was instructed to compose by the general chapter of Narbonne, in 1260, Bonaventure reports that, in the early days of his retirement at La Portiuncula (a chapel dedicated to the Virgin), Francis had great devotion to the Mother of God, "imploring her to be his advocate." She was, moreover, the Queen of virtues and, along with her Son, the prime example of evangelical poverty.

That Francis had a devout piety to Mary is suggested by the report of his early companions, that he used to sing praises to her. One such prayer is included in the critical edition of his works:

Hail, Lady, holy Queen,
holy Forthbringer of God, Mary,
who are a Virgin made Church
and elected by the most holy Father in heaven,
whom He consecrated with his most holy beloved
Son and the holy Spirit, the Paraclete,

in whom there was and is
all the fulness of grace and all good.[6]

Bonaventure, who is not opposed to simple images
or tales that may help popular piety, even tells the story
of a lamb, given to Francis, who would genuflect on
entering the chapel, and bleat before the altar of the
Virgin, "the Mother of the Lamb, as if it wished to
greet her. . . ."

Francis' Marian piety embodied his love for Christ:
"He embraced the Mother of the Lord Jesus with an in-
describable love because she had made the Lord of
Majesty our brother, and because through her we have
obtained mercy. After Christ he put all his trust in her
and made her his advocate and that of his friars." In her
honor he fasted for forty days before the feast of her
Assumption; and he associated her with the angels, since
he also fasted, "out of devotion to the angels," for forty
days after the feast. . . .

Bonaventure was also concerned with the spiritual life
of sisters, especially those who were pursuing the Franciscan ideal of holy poverty on the model of St Francis
and St Clare. One of his works embodies this concern.
The *De Perfectione vitae ad sorores*[7] (*The Perfection of Life
for Sisters*), certainly posterior to the *Threefold Way*, was
composed for a convent which had adopted the rule of
St Clare. According to a tradition that may well be exact,
it was conceived at the request of Isabelle, sister of the
king of France, Louis IX (St Louis). She had founded a
monastery at Longchamp, near Paris, and had chosen
St Clare's ideal for the religious life. This short book is
addressed at times in the singular to the abbess, at times

in the plural to all the sisters. After a brief prologue, it focuses attention, in eight chapters, on eight virtues with which the sisters ought to be familiar: self-knowledge, humility, poverty, silence, desire for prayer, remembrance of the Passion of Christ, love of God, and final perseverance. Allusions to Mary are not numerous; yet they are of importance, located in chapters 2 (humility), 4 (silence), 6 (remembering the Passion), and 8 (final perseverance).

The Virgin Mary is part of what may be called the quadrilateral of humility. Be humble, Bonaventure tells the sisters, "because you have a humble master, our Lord Jesus Christ, and a humble mistress, the Virgin Mary, the queen of all, . . . [and] a humble father, the blessed Francis, . . . [and] a humble mother, the blessed Clare, model of humility."[8] Besides, one should not believe that "virginity pleases God without humility: certainly, Mary would not have been made the Mother of God if she had had pride in her."[9] A nun, often designated here with such appellations as "beloved handmaid of God," "servant of God," should also imitate the Virgin in her silence: "O beloved brides of Jesus Christ, look at your mistress and mine, look at Mary, the mirror of virtues, and learn from her the discipline of silence!"[10] This discipline is manifest in the New Testament, where Mary seldom speaks. "If we go through the gospel, we find that she spoke few words, and with few persons": with the angel, twice; with her Son, twice; with Elizabeth, twice; with the servants at Cana, once. That is all. "In this our loquacity is confounded, for we are inclined to multiplication of words, when great is the usefulness of silence." In a different mode, Bonaventure illustrates the sufferings of Christ in the Passion by reference to the nature of his body. It was not an infrequent notion in medieval piety to insist that, even though he was factually male, Jesus had a qualitatively feminine body, since Mary's virginity entailed that the sole human origin of Christ's body was feminine. This throws light on the Passion:

> See still better how painful the death of Christ was. The more delicate something, the more it suffers. But there never was so delicate a body that had to undergo sufferings as the body of the Savior. For the body of woman is more delicate than that of man; now the flesh of Christ was entirely virginal, because it was conceived of the Holy Spirit and born of the Virgin: therefore the Passion of Christ was the most painful of all passions, since he was the most delicate of all virgins.[11]

The sisters, however, should not meditate only on the Passion. Heaven and eternal blessedness lie ahead of them. "A sweet and most lovable company"[12] is already waiting for them. At the head of it there is of course "Jesus with the Father and the Holy Spirit." Immediately after the Holy Trinity, coming before "the apostles, the martyrs, the confessors, and the heavenly army of all the elect," there is "Mary, with a flower-laden army of virgins."

* * * * *

Most other references to the Virgin Mary in Bona-venture's spiritual writings belong, as was already the case in *The Perfection of Life*, to the literature of meditation. The author illustrates his two basic essays on the spiritual life by providing topics for meditative reading, and images as inducements to the quiet of contemplation. For, as he remarks, "imagination helps understanding."[13]

The *Lignum vitae* (*The Tree of Life*) is a good example in the category of images. It is addressed to "the soul devoted to Christ." The whole program of this small pamphlet is summed up in three invitations: "carefully examine what is said of Jesus, consider it attentively, and reflect on it slowly."

At the beginning, Bonaventure proposes to the reader to imagine a tree, the Tree of Life, which is also the cross of Jesus. The tree has branches; the branches, leaves and fruits. Each branch has four leaves and one fruit. The fruits are placed in three categories, corresponding to the three mysteries of the origin of Christ, of his Passion, and of his glorification. The leaves consistently refer to Jesus. Meditation on them is assisted by a rythmic composition in the form of a hymn or canticle, as for instance, touching the first fruit ("The fame of his origin"):

> Jesus, begotten of God,
> Jesus, fore-announced,
> Jesus, heavenly beam,
> Jesus, born of Mary.[14]

Mary is evoked early in the hymn. After the eternal origin of the Word and the prophecies of the Old Testament about his coming, "Jesus, heavenly beam" reached the Virgin at the Annunciation. Bonaventure again depicts the general framework of the sending of Gabriel to Mary.

At the start of the sixth age of the world (in parallel
with the sixth day of creation, when Adam and Eve were
produced), "the Virgin giving her assent, the Holy Spirit
came upon her like a divine fire which inflamed her
mind and sanctified her flesh with the most perfect
purity."[15] The Word of God took flesh in her. Bonaventure
then, turning to his reader, invites him to sense and to see:

> Oh, if you could somehow feel the quality and the
> power of this fire sent from heaven, of the refresh-
> ment given, of the solace infused, the uplifting of
> the Virgin Mary, the ennobling of humankind, the
> condescension of his Majesty!
> If you could hear the Virgin singing with joy, ascend
> to the mountain with your Lady, see the sweet
> embrace of the sterile woman and the Virgin, and
> the rite of their greeting, in which a servant acknowl-
> edged the Lord, a herald the Judge, a voice the Word—
> I think that you would sing, in sweet modulation,
> the sacred canticle, *Magnificat anima mea Dominum . . .*,
> with the most blessed Virgin, and that, exulting and
> celebrating along with the prophet before the Child,
> you would worship the wonderful conception.

This naturally leads to the last verse, that is, to the
fourth leaf of this first branch: "Jesus, born of Mary."
The birth from Mary closes the stanza, which has been
opened by the eternal begetting of the Word. Bonaventure
depicts the historical context: in the silence "of universal
peace in the emperorship of Caesar Augustus, . . . Joseph,
the Virgin's husband, led the pregnant girl, born of royal
ancestry, to the town of Bethlehem." There, nine months

having elapsed, "this peaceful King proceeded from her virginal womb, brought to the light without corruption, as he had been conceived without the contagion of lust...." This baby, though "great and rich," is now "small and poor, born without the roof of a house, nourished with virginal milk, and lying between an ox and a donkey in a manger." Bonaventure then turns to his own soul:

> Embrace now, o my soul, this divine manger, to touch with your lips and to kiss the feet of the child. Watch in your mind the shepherds' vigils, admire the converging host of angels, join your part to the heavenly melody, singing with heart and mouth: *Gloria in altissimis Deo, et in terra pax hominibus bonae voluntatis.*

Such a presentation has the features of an icon. It functions like a scene in an unfolding play. It is a vignette in the pages of the soul's meditations.

Mary is seen again in the mystery of the Passion, as she illustrates the fruit called "constancy in sufferings":

> Jesus, despised by all,
> Jesus nailed to a cross,
> Jesus, among bandits,
> Jesus, served with gall.

The scene of this last verse brings to Bonaventure's mind a prophetic text which he applies to Mary: "He left me desolate, in pain all the day"[16] (*Lamentations* 1:13). Then he talks to the Virgin, asking her: "What tongue can tell, what intellect can grasp, the weight of your

desolations, O blessed Virgin"? He enumerates the sufferings of the Virgin at the sight of the tortures of her
Son, their many causes and reasons, the several levels of
her soul where she suffered with him, alternately "filled
with gall, shaking, fearing, saddened, agonizing, anxious,
troubled, afflicted by all sadness and sorrow. . . ." The
scene ends with the words of Jesus: "Mother, this is your
son." For Jesus knew that his Mother was "more pierced
by the sword of her compassion" at his sufferings than
if she had borne them in her own body.

* * * * *

In *The Five Feasts of the Child Jesus*, another short work,
Bonaventure borrows images from the Gospels of the
infancy. He introduces us with their help to the very
center of the spiritual tradition of St Francis, who had,
in 1223, started a new Christmas practice by creating a
living crêche, with the help of local people, in the moun-
tainous solitude of Greccio, in the region of Rieti, north-
east of the city of Rome. He is also exploiting a familiar
theme of the Christocentric devotion of the Middle Ages.
Especially under the impact of St Bernard and the
Cistercians, meditation on the humanity of Jesus occupied
the heart of Western Christian spirituality. It was understood that the events of Jesus's life have their counterpart
in the Christian soul. The Franciscan movement tended
to polarize such meditation on the two extreme moments
of the life of Jesus, his infancy and his passion and death.
The reader is thus taken by Bonaventure's meditation
in five points on the childhood of Christ to a deeper level
of the experience of faith. As Bonaventure emphasizes,

the five feasts in question obtain their historical truth from the life of Jesus, yet they have also acquired a spiritual truth in the Christian soul. The step that is envisaged here leads to an interiorization of the mysteries of Christ: these are not only to be believed and accepted; they are also to be lived and experienced in Christian faith and devotion.

Bonaventure's little book is in fact highly personal: the author takes us into his confidence, sharing with his readers his own interior insight:

> While I gradually abandoned the noise of incidental thoughts and I silently meditated within myself on what, at that time, I could in my mind consider of the divine Incarnation, whence I could receive some spiritual consolation, in which, in this vale of tears, I would taste the divine suavity through a mirror, . . . it secretly entered my mind that a soul devoted to God could, by the grace of the Holy Spirit, conceive God the Father's Word and only Son by the power of the Most High. . . .[17]

In other words, the annunciation by the angel is not only made to the Virgin Mary. It is addressed to all faithful souls. This point of departure enables Bonaventure to experience, and then to explain, five moments of the mystic journey, which correspond to the five feasts of the child Jesus: in the faithful and devout soul, (1) Jesus is conceived; (2) he is born; (3) he is named; (4) he is sought and adored on the model of the magi; (5) he is presented to God in the Temple.

Naturally enough, Mary fulfils a role in this spiritualization of the mysteries of Jesus's infancy, since she is the prime scriptural model, who conceives Jesus, from whom he is born, who gives him his name, who welcomes the magi, who presents the child to God in the Temple. In fact, Mary now becomes the model of the soul and, conversely, the soul becomes, spiritually, Mary. Bonaventure now invites the soul, not only to "ascend the mountain with Mary"[18] (as for the visitation), but even to be Mary: "O devout soul, if this delightful nativity pleases you, you must first be Mary."[19] In a sort of dialectical motion, attention shifts from the historical Mary, Mother of Jesus, to the spiritual Mary, the Christian soul, and then again to the historical Mary, who is also spiritual. The Virgin is Jesus's "fortunate natural Mother and true spiritual Mother."[20] This she became when, after giving him his name, Jesus, she "perceived that, in this name, demons were expelled, miracles performed, the blind brought to see, the sick healed, the dead risen."[21] She should therefore serve as model and companion in the mystic journey of the soul as "spiritual Mother."

The name of Mary, as we have already learnt from Bonaventure's biblical commentaries and homilies, means "bitter sea, enlightener, and Lady." But this is precisely the "threefold way" of spiritual ascent:

> Be therefore a bitter sea by contrition. . . . Be secondly an enlightener by your honest conversation. . . . Be thirdly a Lady in control of your senses. . . . Such is the fortunate Mary, who suffers and weeps for past sins, who shines and radiates in virtues, who dominates the lusts of the flesh. From this Mary, Jesus Christ does not despise being spiritually born,

with joy, without pain, without labor. After this fortunate birth, she knows and tastes how sweet the Lord Jesus is.

Finally, the Presentation in the Temple is itself the high point of the spiritual ascent. For going up to the Temple means, for "the spiritual Mary," who at this level is both the holy Virgin and the faithful soul in search of God, to rise up to "the dwellings of the heavenly Jerusalem, to the palaces of the higher city."[22] In this way, when understood and shared spiritually and interiorly, the Presentation in the Temple becomes the ultimate assumption of the soul into the divine presence, before "the throne of the eternal Trinity and undivided Unity."

* * * * *

If the ascent of Mary to the Temple for the presentation of the child Jesus constitutes an image of the assumption of all souls into heaven, another approach, in the form of meditative reading, is offered by Bonaventure in the *Soliloquy*. This is a medieval genre—a dialogue between man and his soul—for which many a model was available in the devotional literature known to the Seraphic Doctor. It is presented, with excessive modesty, as a compilation of sayings of the saints, "for the sake of simple persons, in simple words, in the form of a dialogue, in which a devout soul, the disciple of the eternal Truth, asks questions, and the interior man mentally answers."[23] This booklet is really much more than that. Bonaventure makes available many texts from spiritual authors familiar to him, from St Augustine, St Jerome, St Leo, St Gregory, to St Bernard and Hugh of St Victor. He organizes these excerpts around four basic themes: the contemplation of what is *within* the soul (as created, as damaged by sin, as restored by grace), what is *outside* (the world and its temptations, but also the proper attitude leading to divine consolation), what is *below* (the just punishments of hell), and what is *above* (God and the heavenly court of angels and saints).

The Virgin Mary is briefly evoked in chapter 1, when the soul, looking inside herself, confesses her inability to weep for her sins as she ought. Man, in response, urges her to have recourse to "one of the saints." Quotations from Bernard and Anselm put forward the Mother of God as the one to whom the soul should appeal. But the soul formulates a dilemma: "When I offended the Son, I irked the Mother; and I could not offend her without insulting her Son. What then shall I do, man? Who will reconcile me with the Son, when I am an enemy of the Mother? Who will make me please the Mother, given the wrath of the Son"?[24] The answer, couched in a citation from Anselm, is that both are clement even when offended. Meditation on the outside world and on hell does not bring up the image of Mary. But the Mother of God reappears, in a glorious mode, in the meditation on heaven.

The angels and saints who share the joy of heaven are engaged in a fourfold contemplation (inside, outside, below, above), which should be multiplied by three, each direction bringing up three types of joy. Facing what is *below*, they rejoice in God's victory over evil, in the overcoming of sin in themselves, in their escape from the eternal fire. Facing what is *near*, they rejoice in "the delicious banquet, the beauty of the decoration, the precious treasure gathered by the eternal power."[25] The food of this banquet is a heavenly form of the Eucharist: "this most blessed Lamb, pure and spotless, Jesus, the Son of God the Father and of Mary the Virgin." Facing what is *below*, the saints rejoice in the transformation of the cosmos, its four constitutive elements—earth, water, air, fire—being made into "eternal immortality, universal impassibility, fast agility, and splendid clarity."[26] They also rejoice in the glorification of their own body, which no longer impedes divine contemplation, and in its adornment with all the virtues as with "most precious jewelry." Finally, facing what is *above*, the saints draw joy for their three faculties from the contemplation of the perfect Good in "the mirror of eternity." This is of course the highest contemplation of the three divine Persons. Yet it also includes contemplation of the Mother of God:

O soul, even though these visions alone would be enough if nothing were added, there still remains one—to say nothing of the delightful vision of other all but innumerable realities—which wonderfully brings joy to the minds of all spirits, and which admirably inebriates every blessed creature with I know not what inestimable joy: this is the vision of the deiform radiance of the heavenly Queen and of the glorified humanity of her most blessed Offspring. Who, O my soul, can sufficiently conceive what joy comes from seeing this Mother of mercy, the Queen of piety and clemency, no longer lying with the child who is wailing in the manger, whom all the choirs of angels now serve as their Lady. . . .[27]

Bonaventure continues, contrasting various moments

of the life of Mary with her elevated status, where she is "unmeasurably lifted up above the choirs of angels and every creature, reigning with Christ her Son in the palace of the Trinity."

Once again we have been brought to the summit of contemplation. Yet we have not really reached it, since we are not yet among the saints in heaven. We are left to reflect from afar, to see but in a glass, darkly, in faith, love, and hope. Yet, even so, we can ponder about "the joy, filled with suavity, of seeing the Creator of man as a man, the Woman Forthbringer of the Creator, Jesus our brother, once lost, abject, and despised, but now found, now returned, now reigning, now commanding to all." In the present life, the mystic journey ends in desire, as the soul exclaims:

> O man, I languish in my love to see the Lord God my Creator; I faint in my ardor to behold Jesus my brother and redeemer; I lament, wounded by my desire to contemplate the Virgin Mother.

Notes

1. Prologue, 2. Several translations of the *Itinerarium mentis in Deum* are available, e.g. Philotheus Boehner (with commentary), *Saint Bonaventure's Itinerarium Mentis in Deum*, (St Bonaventure, N.Y.: Franciscan Institute, 1956), José de Vinck, *The Works of Saint Bonaventure*, vol. I: *Mystical Opuscula*, (Paterson, N.J.: St Anthony Guild Press, 1960); Lawrence Cunningham, *The Mind's Journey to God*, (Chicago: Franciscan Herald Press, 1979); Ewert Cousins, *Bonaventure: The Soul's Journey into God; The Tree of Life; The Life of St Francis*, (New York: Paulist, 1978). I have generally used the text of the mystical opuscula as printed in the BAC edition, vol. 2 and 4. De Vinck's translation presents the advantage of containing all the opuscula.

2. Translation in de Vinck, l. c.

3. *Regula novitorum,* in *Selecta Scripta S. Bonaventurae,* 3rd ed., (Quaracchi: Collegio S. Bonaventurae, 1942); citations, ch. 5, n. 2; ch. 1, n. 3.

4. Translation in de Vinck, l. c.; citation, §13.

5. Translation in Ewert Cousins, 1. c., p. 179-327.

6. Regis Armstrong and Ignatius Brady, *Francis and Clare. The Complete Works,* (New York: Paulist, 1982), p. 149-150; I have slightly modified the translation.

7. Text in BAC, vol. 4.

8. Ch. 2, n. 7.

9. Ch. 2, n. 3.

10. Ch. 4, n. 2.

11. Ch. 6, n. 5.

12. Ch. 8, n. 5.

13. *The Tree of Life,* prologue, 2.

14. The entire hymn is inserted after the prologue. The method of meditation requires the formation of an image in the mind; in this Bonaventure anticipates the psychological approaches of later spiritual authors, such as Nicholas of Cusa (*De Visione Dei*) and even St Ignatius with the composition and representation of place, as recommended in the *Exercises.*

15. Fruit I, n. 3-4.

16. Fruit VII, n. 25-28.

17. Prologue.

18. Feast I, n. 3.

19. Feast II, n. 2.

20. Feast III, n. 3.

21. Feast II, n. 2.

22. Feast V, n. 2.

23. Prologue, n. 4.

24. Ch. I, n. 4.

25. Ch. IV, n. 9; 11.

26. Ch. IV, n. 20.

27. Ch. IV, n. 24; 26; 27.

CHAPTER 10

THE LAST SYNTHESIS

In the course of his theological career Bonaventure had to deal with three major crises. Like Thomas Aquinas, he ran into the opposition of a number of secular masters of the university of Paris, who, led by Guillaume de Saint-Amour, in his *Liber de Antichristo*, 1254, and *Tractatus de periculis novissimorum temporum*, 1256, denounced as heretical the doctrine and practice of evangelical poverty that were considered normative in both the Franciscan and the Dominican orders. Guillaume identified such doctrine as a distortion of the gospel, and the friars who espoused it as forerunners of Antichrist and instruments of the coming destruction of the world. In the ensuing controversy, after the interventions of Thomas Aquinas and of the Franciscan Thomas of York, Bonaventure composed his disputed questions *De Paupertate evangelica*, 1256. Guillaume de Saint-Amour was condemned by Pope Alexander IV later in that year. Like Aquinas also, Bonaventure was involved in the debates that flared up later, still at the university of Paris, over the interpretation of Aristotle by Siger de Brabant and his followers in the faculty of arts, a movement that is conventionally called "Latin Averroism." To counter this philosophical trend, which entailed dire consequences for theology, he delivered three series of conferences, the *Collationes de Decem Praeceptis* (1267), *de Donis Spiritus Sancti* (1268), and *in Hexaëmeron* (1273). It is in these special lectures that one finds the last theological synthesis made by the Seraphic Doctor. A third major crisis was peculiar to the Franciscan movement, when the eschatological doctrines of Joachim of Fiore, an abbot of the previous century, were reinterpreted and applied to St Francis by Gerardo di Borgo San Donnino in his *Liber introductorius ad evangelium aeternum,* 1255. Gerardo pursued eschatological projections in straight contradiction to Guillaume de Saint-Amour: St Francis is the angel of the Apocalypse, whose coming heralds the end of the world; the friars, and chiefly the Franciscans, are the "latter-day saints" in whom the Church's ultimate holiness is embodied. Such bizarre notions spread like wild fire. In fact, Bonaventure's election, in 1258, as the superior general of the Franciscans, was largely prompted by the need to counterbalance the Joachimite ideas, shared to some degree by his deposed predecessor, John of Parma.

The *collationes* contain Bonaventure's final teaching concerning the Virgin Mary, the Forthbringer of God. For Mary fits, in the plan of these lectures, at a nodal point. The first series, "On the Ten Commandments," presents a summary of Christian ethics, the basis for the growth in holiness to which all the faithful are called. The second series, "On the Gifts of the Holy Spirit," analyzes the chief instrument of growth in holiness, namely, the gifts through which one may be transformed from sinner into saint. The third series, "On the Six Days of Creation," opens up a transcosmic and eschatological perspective on the Christian faith and life by showing how the present life on earth is tied to, and anticipates, life in heaven with God. In this way, Bonaventure confirms that the "eternal gospel" is already the gospel of Jesus Christ rather than a new message that would have been manifested in Francis of Assisi.

The Virgin Mary is introduced in relation to the gifts of the Holy Spirit, and specifically in the context of the gifts of fortitude and of counsel. These are the fourth and fifth in the traditional listing of the seven gifts: fear of God, piety, knowledge, fortitude, counsel, understanding, wisdom. Thus a first glance already shows that Mary belongs at the center of God's design for creaturely holiness.

The conferences on the gifts constitute a treatise on the nature of divine grace, as it originates in "the Word, through whom all are blessed," as it "descends to humans" through the Word incarnate, crucified, and "in-spired" by the Holy Spirit, and as it comes to fruition in holiness. The treatment of the topic is highly theological. Yet it does not follow the question and debate method of scholasticism. Bonaventure is not in a classroom. His audience is primarily the Franciscans of Paris, and it presumably includes a number of friends and invited guests. The mode of presentation comes close both to that of sermons and to that of commentaries on Scripture: each *collatio* takes the form of a spiritual commentary on a scriptural text, in the course of which Bonaventure brings in other texts to throw light on the main one, constantly appeals to biblical images and quotations, and makes use of some key citations from the theological tradition. His discourse is dialectical, going back and forth between a corporate point of view where the Church is primarily featured, and a personal point of view in which each of the faithful is called to divine grace by divine grace. This twofold perspective is most patent in the treatment of the gift of fortitude, the only one to which two conferences are devoted.

* * * * *

Starting from *Proverbs* 31:10 and 13 ("Who will find a strong woman? . . .), *collatio V* starts with the corporate angle. The strong woman is seen to be the *ecclesia*, but she is also the Virgin:

> Undoubtedly, this has been said to commend mother Church, and specifically to commend the glorious Virgin. In this text she is commended for three things: first, for the solidity of spiritual strength; second, for the fecundity of supernatural conception; third, for the discretion of salutary counsel.[1]

As is often the case in Bonaventure's style, the expression espouses a threefold pattern. The three praises of the strong woman of Scripture are illustrated and explained in three conferences, V to VII. The first—strength —applies primarily to the woman as Church, then as the Virgin (*collatio V*). The second—"supernatural fecundity of conception"—applies to the woman as the "glorious

Virgin" (*collatio VI*). The third—the wisdom of good counsel—applies first to the woman as the Virgin, and next as all the faithful on the way to salvation (*collatio VI*). As one may easily notice, the threefold patterns cover a progressive motion, in which one passes from the corporate dimension (the *ecclesia*) to the private personal one (each faithful), by way of the Virgin Mary, whose place in the design of God is both ecclesial and personal.

All this is contained in "the word of Solomon to the glorious Virgin."[2] It therefore applies to her. Yet the entire fifth conference mentions the Virgin only at the beginning, and speaks directly and explicitly of the Church in describing the inherent strength of the gift of fortitude. This general outline of the *collationes* V to VII tallies with a common idea of medieval theology and spirituality: what is said of the Church is also true of the Virgin; conversely, what is said of the Virgin obtains also for the Church. And since the Church and the Christian soul are not two, but one, the soul of each of the faithful is involved, whether the language is directly ecclesial or Marial. In this perspective, the proper setting for considerations of theology or piety on the Mother of God is the Church, while, at the same time and by the same token, individual Christians are offered, in the image of Mary, a model to imitate and to share.

The Annunciation to Mary, when she accepts the challenge of virginal motherhood of God, highlights her supernatural fecundity. Bonaventure returns here to one of his favorite themes, the Annunciation, as a paradigm of God's relationships with humanity. The price of a strong woman, as the text of *Proverbs* affirms, "comes from far away." This price, originally of course the cost of buying a bride, becomes the price paid for redemption, "the high price which the whole world and the whole humankind had to redeem." In keeping with Anselm's theology of salvation, which is echoed here, such a price could not be paid by created nature alone. "Where," Bonaventure asks, "is this price to be found"? And he answers: "Indeed, nowhere but in the womb of the glorious Virgin." Having next quoted Isaiah's prophecy (in the Vulgate rendition, which, unlike the Hebrew text of Isaiah 7:14, stresses virginity: "A virgin shall conceive . . ."), Bonaventure continues:

> It was not proper for a virgin to have a son unless he be God, or for God to have a mother unless she be a virgin. This price could not be found except in a virgin. It comes indeed from far away, since in it the highest converges with the lowest, the first with the last.[3]

The Christological setting being thus clearly established, Bonaventure now focuses attention on Mary herself:

> To this woman, the blessed Virgin, belongs the price with which we are able to obtain the kingdom of heaven. It is hers, that is, it is taken from her, it is paid by her, and it is owned by her: taken from her in the incarnation of the Word, paid by her in the redemption of the human race, and owned by her in her access to paradisiac glory.

In this threefold relationship to her Son, who is himself

the price of redemption, the Virgin's fortitude acquires three special qualities: "strong and holy, she brought it forth; strong and pious, she paid it; strong and steadfast, she owned it."[4]

The contemplation of these dimensions of Mary's fortitude takes up the rest of *collatio VI*. One may distinguish in it three intermeshing themes: Mary's marriage with God; her recapitulation of Eve; the extension of her motherhood to the faithful.

Bride of God

This theme emerges discretely as Bonaventure speaks of the Annunciation: "To this Virgin Gabriel had to be sent as paranymph."[5] A *paranymphus* (this term was borrowed by the Latin language from the Greek) was, according to the dictionaries, "a young man who accompanied home the bride and bridegroom" during the wedding festivities.[6] In modern customs, we might say that he fulfilled some of the functions of the "best man" at a wedding. If the archangel is a paranymph at the Annunciation, then the Annunciation has to be a nuptial experience. Who was married to whom? As Bonaventure writes, "she alone pleased the Most High." Mary the Virgin became wedded to God. The image of the spiritual marriage, which will be exploited with great effect in the writings of Teresa of Avila and John of the Cross, finds its best and highest application in the Virgin Mary at the Annunciation. As the angel greeted her, Mary was "holy and chaste." She was also "holy with the holiness of prompt obedience."[7] As the angel went on to bless her, she received the Holy Spirit and was made "holy with the holiness of [God's] full benevolence." And this, as Bonaventure draws from the image of wedlock, was an experience of love which the Seraphic Doctor does not shrink from describing with great realism:

> The Holy Spirit is love, and although he is given with his gifts, there is no gift from which he cannot be parted, except the gift of love. For other virtues are common to the good and the evil, and since the love of God and neighbor is proper to the good and pious, [it follows that] love alone sanctifies. The Holy Spirit comes, because love is added to love to transcend the measures of others. . . . The glorious Virgin, bringing forth the Son and the Light of God, gave the light to the world through the fire of divine love, and she was not corrupted. The love of charity preserves from corruption. . . . As a son of the flesh is born from the love of a man with a woman, so from the Virgin's love with God the Son of God was born.[8]

Further on, Bonaventure asks himself: "What made the Virgin conceive"?[9] The question is both theological, touching God's action, and personal, touching Mary's experience. The answer is again borrowed from the nuptiality of the divine love which, in the person of the Holy Spirit, made its dwelling in her: "Indeed it was the Holy Spirit, who is a fervent, fecund, unpolluted, virile, incorrupt, and deifying love." Each of these adjectives has its sign and image in the Old Testament or in nature. Let us note the last three signs: "That it is a virile love is signified for us by woman and man; for woman surrounded man, that is, hemmed him in in every way. That it is uncorrupt love is signified for us in the Virgin, who conceived a Son. That it is deifying love is signified for us in the Virgin begetting God."

Wedlock can serve as an image beyond the event of the Annunciation. Bonaventure sees it again in the Crucifixion, where Mary paid the price of redemption at the foot of the cross. She still experienced her nuptial relationship with God, as she was "strong and pious with compassion for Christ." This compassion was a parturition. Women normally feel pains when they give birth, "before the birth. But the blessed Virgin felt no pains birthing, for she did not conceive from sin . . . , but she felt the pains after birthing. Whence she gave birth before the pains of parturition. In the cross she felt them. . . ."[10] This compassion for Christ was of course spiritual. In a way it was the sword foreseen by Simeon, wielded by the Devil, with which "the soul of the Virgin was pierced." But it was also God's redemptive trick: "She was healed, and the Devil was conquered. The Devil wanted to eat the flesh of Christ; but the Deity clung to his guts like a hook."[11]

The Recapitulation of Eve

This ancient theme of Christian theology is deftly woven into *collatio VI*. It recurs several times, as the principle—that Mary the Virgin undid the harm done by Eve the unvirgin, as Christ undid the harm done by Adam—is variably modulated, in harmony with several moments of Mary's life in which it is at work. "Eve, having transgressed God's mandate, destroyed the gift that God had prepared for our salvation; but the Wise Woman built the house and repaired our salvation."[12] And again, "that woman, namely, Eve, expelled us from paradise and sold us; this one brought us back and bought us": she is "the very strong woman, the uncorrupted Virgin, most obedient and most loving." Once more, as Bonaventure speaks of Mary's post-birthing parturition, he contrasts Mary with "Eve, to whom the curse was given."[13] Following rather closely St Irenaeus, who had developed the theme, Bonaventure sees a contrasting parallel between the shaping of Eve from Adam and that of the Church from Christ. This involves the Church, not only because Mary and the Church are but two aspects of one mystery, but also because the death of Christ was symbolized by the sleep of Adam. "Why," Bonaventure wonders, "does [God] take one of his ribs when he sleeps? Could he not do it while he was awake"?[14]

> This is a mystery. Was not the Church formed from the side of Christ as Christ fell asleep on the cross? And from his side there poured out blood and water, that is, the sacraments through which the Church is reborn. From Adam's rib Eve was formed, who copulated with him in matrimony. As man was formed from the virginal earth, so Christ from the glorious Virgin. And as from the side of the sleeping Adam the woman was formed, so the Church from Christ hanging from the cross. And as from Adam and Eve Abel and his successors were formed, so from Christ and the Church the whole Christian people.

This ecclesial perspective enlarges the process of

recapitulation beyond the contrasting pair, Mary and
Eve. Mary also recapitulates many of the women of the
Scriptures, who by their deeds or their words heralded
or represented her. Judith stands in good place. This is
paradoxical, since she used the sword to kill Holofernes,
and Mary never committed a bloody deed. "How does
Judith signify the glorious Virgin? See the New Testament
and the Old."[15] The Virgin used a sword, the sword of
her sorrow in the Passion of Christ; and the Devil was
caught! From the New Testament the image of Mary
Magdalen stands out: she, the type of penitents, "broke
the vase of perfume out of her piety toward Christ."[16]
Having lost God by her offenses, "when she anointed
the feet and the head of Christ, she found him." Mary,
who is unlike the Magdalen in regard to doing penance,
is still like her. For, as Magdalen gave up her expensive
perfume, so Mary, "being strong and holy, brought out
the price, and, being strong and pious, paid it." Ending
this trilogy of unique women, Esther the queen is recapitulated in the Virgin's glory. "Esther found grace
before Assuerus above all other women, and he placed
a diadem on her head and made her the queen."[17] Likewise, "the blessed Virgin, for her holiness, piety, and
sublimity, had a crown of precious stone. What is this
stone? It is certainly Christ." The Virgin was crowned
with Christ in both flesh and spirit, as "in her flesh she
saw the body of Christ glorified, in her spirit his soul
glorified, and in her mind his divinity."

Mary brought to light the meaning of the feminine
symbols of the Old and the New Testaments:

Anna, who offered Samuel, was praised. . . . She

offered her son for service; but the blessed Virgin offered her Son in sacrifice. Abraham wished to offer his son, but he offered a he-goat, while the glorious Virgin offered her Son. The poor widow is praised, for she offered all she had; but this woman, the glorious Virgin, most merciful, pious, and devoted to God, offered all her substance.[18]

Bonaventure does not even shrink from the idea that there was an image of Mary in "the strong woman and her price, whom Solomon desired,"[19] and another in the woman and the man of whom Jeremiah said that woman will surround man. "All this was consummated in the glorious Virgin." In a sense, it is not only individual, typical women who are recapitulated in the Virgin; it is also womanhood. But recapitulation implies both bringing to perfection and correcting. Conceiving and birthing were recapitulated in the Annunciation and the Passion. "In other women there is the pain of the flesh, in her the pain of the heart; in others the pain of corruption, in her the pain of compassion and charity."[20] In marriage, "the hands of woman are tied to those who touch them, since it is strictly held that man cannot be separated from her."[21] But one can remain free by following the Virgin.

Mother of the Faithful

One should readily admit that this is not a frequent theme in the works of Bonaventure. It is even rare. Yet it should not be neglected, because, if the notion that Mary is in some sense a mother to the faithful does not function as a principle in Bonaventure's Mariology, it has the quality of a conclusion. It sums up a point which he regards as important, namely, that the faithful must follow Christ and, in so doing, will imitate the Virgin through whom the Lord came to them. This itself derives directly from the contrasting parallel between Eve and Mary.

"Not only is she blessed, the one who conceived and breast-fed him, but also those who follow her. And who are these? They are those who hear the word of God and fulfil it."[22] Thus is Mary's response to the angel the key to her whole life and to that of all the faithful. These formulate their own *fiat* on the model of hers. And such a *fiat* cannot remain an isolated moment at the beginning of the life of faith; it must be constantly renewed in the everyday actions of one's life. This was the case with Mary, for she heard the word of God and fulfilled it. "Everyone who wants to be holy must follow the glorious Virgin in the holiness of uncorrupted chastity, of prompt obedience, and of full benevolence."[23] Bonaventure becomes personal as he then addresses Eve and her descendants:

> Stupid Eve, for eating one apple you sold yourself, and your husband, and all of us! O child of Eve, take care not to be imitator of Eve; and for whatever pleasure you give your soul, you are the imitator of Eve . . .—For all that God created I would not give my soul!—Christ gave his blood for the redemption of your soul, and for a sin you sell yourself and your soul!

Bonaventure is then led to an unusual interpretation

of the words of Jesus on the cross, "This is your son. . . . This is your Mother." He has just remarked that Mary did consent to Jesus' self-offering to the Father for the sins of humankind: "She agreed that the price of her womb be offered for us on the cross."[24] Then, as Jesus saw his Mother with the other women and with his disciple,

> he said to his Mother: "Woman, this is your Son," that is, "who is being exchanged as the price of the redemption of humankind"; as though he said: "It is opportune that you miss me, and that I miss you"— and you yourself in holiness conceived him and in piety offer him up; "may you agree, O Virgin, that I redeem humankind and that I please God." And, lest she be destitute, he told the disciple: "This is your Mother." He gave the Virgin a virginal man.

Thus understood, the word from the cross does not designate the faithful as Mary's sons and daughters. Jesus remains her only Son. He wished his mother, at that point of his agony, still to recognize him as indeed her Son, and thus to suffer with himself. In the process, by an afterthought which was not essential to the main point, but which expressed Jesus' last human care for his mother, the disciple whom Jesus loved was given a mother to look after. It is therefore not through a spiritual reading of this text that Bonaventure concludes to a symbolic motherhood of Mary for the faithful. Only a further extension of the parallel Eve-Mary leads the Seraphic Doctor to this point: "As Eve is the mother of Abel and of all of us, so the Christian people has the Virgin as its mother."[25] Having said this, Bonaventure is able to exclaim:

> Oh, what a pious mother we have! Let us imitate our mother and follow her piety. Such compassion had she for souls that she held temporal condemnation and corporal suffering for nothing. May it thus please us to crucify our body for the salvation of our soul.

The ties that are thus established between Mary and the faithful do not end there. Imitation is only a beginning. There was also, for the Virgin, as we have seen, a crowning with the stone which was Christ. The first crowning, however, was for Christ himself as he entered the heavens through his Resurrection and Ascension. The second crowning was for her: "First Christ was crowned, and, after him, she was."[26] His crowning was the glorification that ensued his Incarnation and his Passion: "He first put on the flesh, and suffered, and afterwards he was glorified; and the whole Church was crowned through him." The word, assumption, is not used at this point. Yet the Virgin's glorification through Christ corresponds to what the feast of her Assumption was meant to celebrate. What Bonaventure now envisions is a glorification, an assumption, of the whole Church through Christ. Mary, in her own glorification, is not the instrument of it, but she remains a model for it. And this model has a message for all those who believe: "We shall have this crown, if we want to imitate the glorious Virgin."

Collatio VII starts again, like *collatio V* and *VI*, with the verse of Proverbs: "Who will find a strong woman"? The strong woman is "the glorious one who found Wisdom in herself and who brought it forth to the world." In fact, however, the Virgin is explicitly mentioned only at the beginning of the lecture, the bulk of which, after Bonaventure's words, "Let us speak about counsel,"[27] explains, with examples and biblical illustrations, the nature and function of the gift of counsel.

The mention of the Virgin takes the form of a popular story about a "white monk," that is, a Cistercian. This man "had a good will toward the glorious Virgin; every day he said to her a psalter of one hundred and fifty *Hail Marys*; but he was hard-headed."[28] One may remark that one hundred and fifty is the count of the rosary in its final form: three times five decades. But there is no indication here of a division in decades: this is "a psalter," that is, a prayer of praise, similar to the one (of one hundred only) which Bonaventure had recommended earlier to the Franciscan novices. Be that as it may, the story goes on to explain that, when the monk was about to die, the Devil had good reason to claim him; but the Virgin claimed him too. What tipped the scale toward her was that, as the Devil simply demanded justice, Mary asked her Son for a drop of his blood; she placed it on the side of the monk's meager merits. And down went the scale: the result was not contested. The Devil admitted his defeat as he said to the Virgin: "It is not good to fight with you." All that the Devil could gain was the authorization to afflict the poor man in his last bodily illness. The story comes, Bonaventure affirms, from the monk himself as he was able to confess his sins to the abbot before dying. "And, having shown a noble compunction, he went to the Lord, and this suffering counted as his purgatory."

This kind of tale, one should remember, was told in many a miracle-play of the Middle Ages. In fact, the cathedral of Paris, Notre-Dame, which was started in 1150 and completed about one century later, was itself dedicated to the Virgin. The portal of its north transept, which was decorated around 1250, when Bonaventure was in Paris, featured a similar legend: the saving by Mary of Theophilus, a cleric who had sold his soul to the Devil. . . . Both Bonaventure and his audience must have been familiar with the story and with the sculpture. How much of this Bonaventure really believed I do not think one can ascertain. How well his version of it could please the Cistercian monks is also something one may wonder about. At any rate, Bonaventure was no more loathe to illustrate his teaching with popular legends than he was to discover allegorical meanings in holy Scripture. But what exactly is the point of the story as he tells it? It is not that Mary herself saves, or claims something that does not properly pertain to her, or fights the strict demand of divine justice with the generosity of her love. It is that, at Mary's prayer, the sinful monk was saved by the blood of Jesus. Jesus saves. But it is the right of Mary, and of all the faithful, to pray.

* * * * *

Bonaventure's final words on the Virgin Mary are spoken in the lectures on the *Hexaëmeron*. This is not by way of lengthy considerations, but in occasional allusions. The predominantly ecclesial and eschatological tone of this last major work of the Seraphic Doctor called for another focus than the Virgin: Bonaventure is not now engaged in gauging the full import of the Annunciation, though, in his very last word, he will touch on the topic.

Mary does appear from time to time in the grandiose theological fresco that Bonaventure is now painting. For she, "who touched the Word in her womb and her tenderness," is, as stated in *collatio IX*, "teacher (*Doctrix*) of the apostles and evangelists."[29] She is intimately related to the allegorical meaning of Scripture, which is described symbolically in Ezechiel's vision (Ez 1:6). Scripture has, like the animals of the vision, four faces or senses. In turn, the allegorical sense has four faces. The first is Christological, the second Mariological, the third ecclesial, and the fourth is scriptural, when Scripture refers to itself. Of these four faces the first is of course predominant. It relates to "the humanity assumed, in its nativity and its passion, which are the principal allegories." The second, however,

> is the Mother of God, Mary, since beautiful things are said of her in Scripture, since in all the Scriptures she is featured in relation to her Son. And what some people say—why are so few things said of the blessed Virgin?—is nonsense: for many things are said, since there is something about her everywhere, and more is said of her everywhere than if one wrote a treatise. The third is the Church militant, or Mother-Church, which receives many praises in Scripture. . . .[30]

As this reasoning implies, the ubiquity of Mary in Scripture derives from the ubiquity of Christ: where he is, she is. The language of Scripture applies universally to her Son, and, through him, by way of redundance, also to her. Christ is the sun; she is a "vase receiving the sun, a vase admirable like the sun."[31] In Mary's life one sees the cosmic design of God at work for her Son. After twelve years of universal peace, when "the Temple of Peace in Rome was closed," the emperor ordered a description of the world to be made: "God put it in the heart of this pagan, so that the Virgin would go to Bethlehem and there give birth in a manger."[32]

For the faithful who are seeking for living examples of faith, however, the full impact of the image of the Virgin is not there. It is found once more in what happened at the Annunciation, when Mary believed. "If you wish for an example of faith, [Scripture shows you] Abraham and the glorious Virgin, whose faith transcended Abraham's faith. For Abraham believed that he could have a son from a sterile womb; but Mary believed that a virgin would conceive from the Holy Spirit. Had she not believed, she would not have conceived."[33]

In this way the last word of Bonaventure on the Virgin Mary extols the power and the necessity of faith.

Notes

1. *Coll.* VII, n. 1; I have used the BAC edition, vol. V.

2. *Coll.* VI, n. 1.

3. *Coll.*, VI, n. 4; 5. The convergence of the highest with the lowest cannot be properly assimilated to a "coincidence of opposites"; for Bonaventure, along with the other schoolmen of his time, explicitly denies the possibility of a coincidence of opposites: G. Tavard, *The Coincidence of Opposites: a Recent Interpretation of Bonaventure* (*Theological Studies*, vol. 41, n. 3, Sept. 1980, p. 576-584).

4. l. c., n. 5.

5. l. c., n. 6.

6. L. Quicherat, *Thesaurus Poeticus Linguae Latinae*, Paris, 1875, p. 783.

7. l. c., n. 7.

8. l. c., n. 8.

9. l. c., n. 11.

10. l. c., n. 18.

11. l. c., n. 23.

12. l. c., n. 7; 14.

13. l. c., n. 18.

14. l. c., n. 20.

15. l. c., n. 23.

16. l. c., n. 21.

17. l. c., n. 24.

18. l. c., n. 17.

19. l. c., n. 9.

20. l. c., n. 18.

21. l. c., n. 14.

22. l. c., n. 7.

23. l. c., n. 12.

24. l. c., n. 15.

25. l. c., n. 20; 21.

26. l. c., n. 24.

27. *Coll.* VII, n. 4.

28. l. c., n. 3.

29. *Coll.* IX, n. 13; a translation of the *In Hexaëmeron* is included in de Vinck, l. c., vol. 5.

30. *Coll.* VII, n. 20.

31. *Coll.* XIII, n. 27.

32. *Coll.*, XVI, n. 16.

33. *Coll.*, IX, n. 9.

CONCLUSION

The most notable point about Bonaventure's theological perspective on Mary, as I see it at the end of the present enquiry, relates to the differences in tone and vocabulary that are found in the several parts of his works. One may say that each of the four sections of this book features a special theology of the Virgin Mary, objective and more intellectual in Bonaventure's scholastic writings, warm and more imaginative in his scriptural commentaries, devotional and more triumphalistic in his liturgical preaching, meditative and more interior in his spiritual opuscula and his final lectures. Bonaventure the theologian goes one way; Bonaventure the poet and orator takes another way. Yet, just as they are one person, the corresponding Mariologies are profoundly one at the core: they all turn around reflection on the central event of Mary's life, the Annunciation. At the four levels of the Seraphic Doctor's thought and expression regarding Mary, the Mother of the Savior is seen as the one who welcomes the angelic message. In her *fiat*, she commits herself body and soul to the divine purpose for her and for humanity. The archangel's word, "highly favored one"—if this is a good rendering of the Greek term, *checharitomene*—encapsulates the highest theology about the Virgin. It is in Mary's acceptance of this address that she becomes the indispensable instrument of the Incarnation, the Forthbringer of God. At that moment, the "Handmaid of the Lord" is made, by divine grace, the Bride of God.

Christian reflection is one thing. Christian piety, while related to it, is another thing. From the mere standpoint of rational simplicity, the position of John Duns Scotus on the Immaculate Conception is neater and makes better sense than the previous, rather messy, description of Mary's first sanctification in her mother's womb shortly after her conception. But piety and devotion do not need the kind of clinical detail that was discussed by the Scholastics in this regard. It should be enough to accept the divine plan, even if one cannot be fully acquainted with it, and is never able, in any case, fully to understand what is known of it. All that is ultimately called for is a delicate sensitivity to the meaning of the Annunciation and to the mind of the young girl who is, with her consent, thrown by it into the hands of the Living God.

Whether we believe that the modern Marian definitions have come at the ripe moment or, as I would rather think, that they were both unnecessary and inopportune, we should appreciate Bonaventure's implicit reminder, that these aspects of the Mother of God may be seen in another light than the one which the recent formulations of the doctrine have stressed. The sinlessness of the Virgin, which Bonaventure certainly taught, does not derive from her, but from God's prevenient grace: it embodies the divine will to elevate the lowly, to justify the unjust. As such, the Immaculate Conception is not a "privilege," the spiritual counterpart of "miracles": it is, as Martin Luther might have said (but I am not aware he said it) a sermon on justification by faith. Likewise, Mary's Assumption into heaven after she died (for, being subject to the condition of humanity, she must, like her Son, have died) should not be seen as a miraculous happening special to her: it embodies the destiny of the *Ecclesia*, and of all the faithful, to be taken, after death, into another mode of existence, in God. The doctrines are icons, images, of the ultimate reality present in Christ, windows into the heart of things, or projections of the *Ecclesia*. The Church is the primary category, and the all-encompassing context, in which Mary is placed as the most central specific creaturely image, pointing to the divine Word.

Perhaps at some future time the three main directions of Christian existence and thought—Orthodox, Catholic, Protestant—will be able to reformulate jointly the heart of their faith, and to assess in similar ways the radiation of it into the creaturely realm: from Christ as the Word made flesh at the center, to the consequences and implications of his coming and his abiding with the Church in the Holy Spirit, to the transformation of the creaturely world, of humanity and of matter, to the glory of the Father. At that moment, Bonaventure will be spiritually present, along with his older reflection on the Forthbringer of God.